STEAMING INTO THE WEST

More Tales of Western Steam

Michael Clutterbuck

HEDDON PUBLISHING

First edition published in 2025 by Heddon Publishing.

Copyright © Michael Clutterbuck 2025, all rights reserved.
No part of this book may be reproduced, adapted, stored in a retrieval system or transmitted by any means, electronic, photocopying, or otherwise without prior permission of the author.

ISBN 978-1-917824-13-2 (paperback)
978-1-917824-14-9 (ebook)

Cover design by Heddon Publishing.

Cover image courtesy of Lawrence Waters of the Great Western Trust.

This is a work of fiction. Names, characters, businesses, places, events and incidents are either the products of the author's imagination or used in a fictitious manner. Any resemblance to actual persons, living or dead, or actual events is purely coincidental.

www.heddonpublishing.com
www.facebook.com/heddonpublishing

William Harold Clutterbuck
1901 - 1979

Known to his family as Harold and at his work as Bill, our father followed his father, a driver, and his older brother Trevor, into the Great Western Railway. Dad worked in a clerical capacity and passed into British Railways, Western Region, in 1948, retiring, with a gold watch, after forty-five years of railway service in the early 1960s. Being in a 'reserved occupation', he was prevented from joining the army at the beginning of the Second World War, so he joined the Air Raid Precautions service, and we children hardly saw him during the week as he was at work with the GWR during the day and out with the ARP at night. Additionally, he won a medal for his voluntary work in the National Savings Certificate Scheme. Shortly after the end of the War in 1947, our mother left him with three small children, aged ten, eight and four, to bring up on his own, which he managed very well, seeing us all married and off his hands. To our great pleasure, he lived long enough to see all his ten grandchildren, even the two out here Downunder during two visits. He died peacefully in his sleep in his house, looked after by his elder daughter. He was a quiet and patient man who was loved by his children and grandchildren, and also highly respected by his friends and work colleagues.

Introduction

This, the last of the Steaming Into series of books, shows an inclination to favour the western side of the UK. There are good reasons for this. My father was a Great Western Railway timetable clerk. He joined the GWR around 1920, retiring from his GWR/BR(W) service with a gold watch in 1964. He married in 1936 and bought himself some GWR Hornby trains in case he acquired a son to play with them. I arrived in 1937 (rather earlier than approved of in those days), and those Hornby trains played a very large part in my youthful entertainment during the war.

My paternal grandfather had joined the Great Western Railway in 1881, retiring as a Shrewsbury driver in 1922. My father's older brother joined the GWR around 1913 but left again in 1915, when sent to Australia by his mother to prevent his conscription into the British army. (He joined the Australian army, was sent to Europe, got shot in the leg and met his mother again in a London hospital less than a year after she had sent him to safety.)

My sisters and I had access to Privilege tickets; issued to railway staff and their dependants and which cost about a third of the regular price, so during our formative years in the 1940s and 1950s we travelled everywhere by train, mostly on the Western. In the summer of 1959, I even briefly worked for the Western Region in Chester's General Station, in a summer clerical job. I have been an avid, if mediocre, GWR modeller most of my life. With such a railway background, where else could my allegiance possibly lie?

Readers of the Steaming Into series will find a few familiar names appearing in this book as more incidents involving them are related.

With this series of railway stories, there are several people I am deeply indebted to. Initially, my good friend Dr John Ritter, who suggested I publish my first little tale and continued to give his technical and valuable advice throughout the series. Lawrence Waters of the Great Western Trust has been kind enough to send me photos for some of the book covers. Kath Smith, my editor, has continually encouraged me, overseeing the books and improving them immensely through her advice and generous support. Most important of all is my wife Christa; she first urged me to bite the bullet and publish the first book, and has continued to put up with my retiring to the computer to write yet another title in the series when I ought to have been doing the weeding or peeling the spuds.

Mike Clutterbuck. Melbourne, 2025

CONTENTS

1 - Dragons? Be Here Dragons? (June 1819) 1
2 - A Wider Wisdom (Sept 1833) 10
3 - The Western Makes its Mark (Sept 1841) 19
4 - It Pays to Watch the Time (March 1852) 28
5 - The Thin End of the Wedge (Feb 1861) 37
6 - Cornish Confusion (May 1877) 46
7 - "How are the Mighty Fallen!" (Feb 1881) 55
8 - The New Broom (Oct 1901) 64
9 - The Mighty Monarchs (June 1927) 73
10 - Driver Denton's New Mate (April 1936) 82
11 - Beginner's Luck? (June 1940) 91
12 - There's no Safety at Home (April 1941) 100
13 - Lance Shirks a Duty (Nov 1941) 109
14 - Driver Smith and the Brigadier (May 1944) 119
15 - The War Ends (June 1945) 129
16 - 'I Don't Feel No Different!' (Dec 1947) 138
17 - Do Britannias Rule the Rails? (May 1953) 147
18 - A Taunton Trauma (July 1960) 156
19 - Flagging the Change (Feb 1961) 165
20 - The Sun Sets in the West (Oct 1965) 175
Glossary of Technical Railway Terms 185
GWR Running Sheds Town Running Shed codes 188

1 - Dragons? Be Here Dragons? (June 1819)

The stagecoach was rattling along at a fine rate with an elderly gentleman and a young boy as passengers inside. The gentleman pulled his gold watch out of his waistcoat and glanced at it.

"We'll be home in an hour, young George, and you'll be back in the bosom of your family once again, after your short break. It's holiday time and you'll be away from that school you are so fond of!"

George, aged twelve, smiled at his companion's little joke; he hated his school, as Colonel Mayhew knew very well. Mayhew was an ex-army officer and a business friend of the family, accompanying George back home from a weekend away.

"The lessons and even some of the teachers are quite interesting, sir," George said. "The problem is when the bigger boys hold us in front of a fire to punish us for not doing things for them when we have schoolwork to do. Then we get punished again by our teachers because we haven't done the work they have required of us. It's really quite unfair!"

"What about the schoolwork itself? Do you enjoy any particular lessons more than others?"

"I do like languages," mused George, "but Father doesn't hold with Latin and Greek; he asks what use are dead languages that nobody uses? He wants me to study engineering and mathematics."

The colonel sighed. "I believe your father is partly right about Greek; it is important, but only for those who study the past. Latin is important in law, of course, and it also gives us an insight into the origin of the meaning of many words in our language. Yet engineering and mathematics are the studies for the future; I am with him there in every respect. And George, from what you say about bullying in schools, I don't believe much has changed since I was a boy. I had the same trouble and we—" He stopped as the stagecoach suddenly shuddered to a halt, the sound of shouting coming from outside.

George peered out of the open window and pulled his head quickly back inside again. He had caught sight of a man on a horse, aiming what looked like two pistols at the coachman.

"I think there's a highwayman outside!" he gasped, just as a shot rang out.

"Is there indeed?" growled the colonel. "Get down on the floor, George, quickly!" George did as he was told and the colonel reached into a bag, pulling out a pistol of his own, loading it quickly with powder and ball and tamping the ball down in the barrel. He slipped the weapon into his bag and waited.

Shortly, the door was torn open and a heavily bearded man holding a pistol stared in to see how many people he could steal from. His face showed disappointment when he saw there were only two passengers, and one was a young boy.

"Look what you have done, sir; the boy is frightened!" the colonel snapped at the highwayman. "He's cowering on the floor! Have you no manners?"

"Shut yer gob, Granfer, jist open yer bag and give us wot's inside!" snarled the man waving his pistol in a threatening manner. "An' then I'll 'ave wot's in yer pockets!"

"It seems I have no choice." Colonel Mayhew slowly opened his bag and, while the highwayman's eyes gleamed in anticipation, the colonel pulled out his pistol and shot the would-be robber in his hand. As the man screamed in pain and fell back, dropping his own weapon, Mayhew slammed the door shut and quickly began to reload his gun but there shortly followed the sound of further moaning outside and then racing hooves as the highwayman apparently raced away.

"You can rise, George. I think we shall see whether the coachman has been hurt. We may be somewhat late home tonight, if I have to take the reins."

The coachman was not hurt but he was badly frightened. "'E come out o' the bushes, sir, wavin' a pistol at me. 'E 'ad another in 'is 'and an' 'e shot one of 'em past me face. I 'ad ter stop sharpish like."

"Then you have come to no harm, Coachman?"

"No, sir, thanks to yer pistol. 'E raced orf moanin' sumthin' dretful!"

As the coach moved off again, the colonel and George settled back inside the coach.

"You were very quick with your pistol, sir," remarked George.

The colonel picked up the weapon that the highwayman had dropped and unloaded it skilfully. "Fighting the French under General Amherst in Quebec and Montreal, even as an officer, you had to pick between what the Good Book calls the 'Quick and the Dead', George. I chose to be among the Quick. Alas," he sighed, "I am no longer sufficiently quick for the present fighting of the French in Europe."

"Are the French bad men, sir?"

Mayhew paused. "No worse than us, George, no worse than us; but their government is a different matter. Before Canada, I spent time in Russia, Prussia and Hanover, and I learned that although people speak different languages," he shook his head, "they're not really different, not even the Indians of North America. Remember that!"

George nodded. "Our teacher told us of a French engineer who built a machine which could move on its own without a horse, sir. He said it could pull a canon in battle. It sounded like a fine idea."

"Yes, it is an admirable concept. That man's name was Nicholas Cugnot, and his machine had problems with its guidance, which is a minor matter, but the French have been foolish not to study the idea in more detail. Regrettably," the colonel added, "our own engineers are not well endowed mentally either. That device has great promise, but our leaders appear blind to its possibilities."

"I have sometimes wondered, sir," George reflected cautiously, in case his companion should think this just childish supposition, "whether an improved machine engine of that kind could run on wooden rails, or iron perhaps, if it's heavy, and pull loads of coal for long distances."

Mayhew looked at the boy in surprise and smiled, a glint of approval in his eyes.

"And-" continued young George continued with a slight smile - "if they could carry people, they might be running too fast for highwaymen, or they could carry soldiers as guards?"

A smile spread gradually over the colonel's face.

"You'll go far, young Master Stephenson," he remarked. "Other great minds are thinking along those lines. Have you put that thought to your father yet?"

***

It was quiet in the little house halfway up the valley. The children's mother was in the field, milking the cow; their father was out at work and wouldn't be home until dark, and the three children were on their own for a few minutes. The youngest – Sarah, aged five – was studying a picture of a dragon in her book. She couldn't yet read of course; her mother read the words, but Sarah liked to look at the pictures. Her brother Jeb, two years older, was nibbling a carrot, and their nine-year-old cousin Jamie, visiting from across the Scottish border, was gazing around the house, visibly bored.

He glanced over to Sarah. "Whit're lookin' at, Sarah?"

Sarah held her book up so that Jamie could see the picture. "It's me dragon."

"Aye, but there's nae dragons noo; they're all deid."

"But I seed a live one."

"Ye've seen one? Nae, ye canna have seen one. There hav'nae been dragons fer thousands of yeers."

"But I seed one!"

"Och, I telled ye, they're all deid. Yer on'y a bairn; whit would ye know aboot dragons?"

Jeb was listening, and he smiled to himself: he had an idea.

He stood up. "Coom wi' me, bonny lad, an' leave Sarah ter t'book."

Jamie nodded and stood up, thankful to be doing something. He followed Jeb out of the house. The cousins didn't see each other too often.

"I'll tek yer fer a little walk and show ye summat." Jeb's Geordie accent sounded different from Jamie's broad Scots. Jeb took Jamie down the valley and into a little copse, where they crouched behind a large bush. Jeb said nothing but put his finger to his lip for silence.

"Whit're we lookin' fer?" whispered Jamie

"Wait an' see."

They waited until a strange coughing sound gradually made itself heard, growing louder as it approached. With its strange gasping, this did not sound like any animal Jamie had ever come across. As it came ever closer to where the two boys were hiding, the hairs on the back of his neck began to rise and he saw what seemed to be smoke arising from the beast's direction. His mind flicked to images from little Sarah's book of dragons with smoke and fire spouting out of their mouths, and he crouched lower, in terror. Jeb, squatting behind his cousin, eyes gleaming in mischief, watched Jamie's dread mounting, until the boy's horrified eyes took in the sight of what seemed to be a huge, bulbous beast with a long horn spouting smoke and a distinct glimpse of fire in its body. Then, with a roar, it burst forth in front of them, dragging a long, jerking tail behind it.

Jamie's horrified screech echoed around the valley as he leapt up and raced off back the way they had come, his cousin shaking with laughter and trotting behind until they reached the farm.

Jeb's mother looked up in surprise from her milking when she saw her nephew hurtling past. "What's with Jamie, Jeb?"

"'E's just seen 'is first rail road injin, Ma, an' thinks 'e's seen a dragon!"

"Och, yer an evil lad, Jeb, frightenin' yer cousin like that!" She carried on with her milking with a chuckle.

A shaken Jamie ran into the house where Sarah looked up from her picture. "Jamie? What's up wi' ye?"

Jeb came in, chortling. "'E's just seen yer dragon, an' 'e's cacked in his trews!"

But by this time, Jeb's laughter and his aunt's unworried reaction had eased Jaimie's initial fright, and the insult finally brought him back to reality.

"Ah have not!" he claimed indignantly. "Ah was jist surprised. Whit was it?"

"That were our dragon; it's a mechanical injin machine wot brings the coal chaldrons down the 'ills ter't'coast; it comes down this 'ere rail-road three times a day wi't'coal and goes back up wi't'empty chaldrons. It'll be back in an hour, so I'll tek yer ter see it agen if yer not afeard."

"Aye, Ah'll come with yer. Ah've nivver seen a meechanical-" (he pronounced it slowly) – "*injin* afore that moves on its own."

Jamie now recalled mention of such machines in mines, which could pump out foul air and replace it with fresh; and he had heard that similar engines could help in mills, grinding corn or weaving cloth, but he had never seen one. There was nothing like that near his father's farm deep in the Scottish hills.

An hour later, the boys were settled in full sight of the rail-road (as Jeb called it), and they heard the distant sound of the engine approaching. This time it was not so loud because the chaldrons were empty. Jamie gasped as he saw the engine more clearly, running along twin rails. It was a huge, round drum with a chimney, on four wheels: two big ones in front and two small ones behind them, and two men standing on a shelf at the back.

One man was holding a tall lever and the other leaned forward and opened a hole in the back of the drum before turning to fill a shovel with coal from a box on wheels behind and throw it into the hole. Bright flames were visible within and there was smoke puffing out from the tall tube at regular intervals, and steam emerging from other places, giving the machine a live and fearsome appearance. Jamie could see why he had been so shocked the first time he saw it. What he had thought of as its swaying tail was in fact a row of a dozen or so wagons being hauled along.

Noticing the boys, the man with the lever waved cheerfully at them as the engine passed by.

"That's Harry Bolton; he works the injin," explained Jeb. "Me dad an' 'im are friends."

"An' the other man?"

"'E stokes the fire ter keep the steam goin'."

"Why don't they use horses tae pull the chaldrons?"

"One injin c'n pull thirty ton o' coal. Ye'd need a lot o' 'orses ter do that!"

"Aye," said Jamie thoughtfully. "Ah c'n see that."

"An' sometimes ye c'n see the chaldrons wi' people in 'em!"

"People in 'em? Whit for?"

"Comin' 'ome wi' their shoppin' from down in t'village."

"But the chaldrons'll be dirty wi' all the coal!"

"Aye, they are, but if ye've a 'eavy bag an' four-mile ter carry it, a bit o' dirt isna goin' ter stop yer gettin' 'elp!"

"Is it free?"

"Nay, they pays a penny, but the injin don't care if the chaldrons're 'eavy or empty, so the men get money fer doin' nowt more'n what they allus do!"

"That cannae be right," muttered Jamie. "Money fer doin' nuthin'?"

"Nuthin' *more*! They gotta work the injin any'ow, wi' a load o' people or coal; it don't matter to the injin, so if there's people in their train, the men get more money." Jeb poked Jamie, smiling at the simple logic.

Jamie frowned, looking at the rail-road, "Aye, ye're right." He was thinking that his younger cousin might be a rich man one day. His own parents had put him in a carriage with five or six other people, and two horses had drawn it from Scotland down to Northumberland in a day. Could people be really taken around the country on one of these rail-roads one day? A rail-road engine could obviously take far more people than even an expensive coach and four, and no need to change horses every twenty miles. He decided he would have another look at this rail-road machine every chance he had before he returned home to the quiet farm in Scotland.

***

"I'm right glad I married yer, Lil!" The young leatherworker looked fondly at his new wife. They were standing near the Liverpool and Manchester Railway with a crowd of other people, watching the procession of trains at the opening ceremony.

"Yer might be a furrinner, but by Gor, yer c'n cook!" added Alfred Hardman. "What were that wot we et yesterday?"

"We haf it much at home; mine mutter cook it. We say Labskaus and it iss much in Hamburg eaten. It iss cheap and taste good."

"Aye, well yer c'n cook it as much as yer like!"

"But Alfred, what we do here today? You work not!"

"No, Harry's lookin' after the shop. I'm just takin' yer fer a day out ter see the new trains!"

Lilly peered through the crowd to see the first train. There were many people sitting in the wagons and cheerful black and yellow coaches. Vehicles with coal and water carts were lined up to re-supply the locomotives. Pie-sellers were everywhere and there was a festival atmosphere with spectators eager to watch this fascinating display; nothing quite like this had ever been seen before. There were tracks with several trains to see, one of them coming from the Liverpool direction and beginning to slow down to stop.

"I think they're goin' ter put more coal in ter get 'em to Manchester, Lil," remarked Alfred, and he pointed in excitement. "An' look, that's the Duke; 'e's our prime minister!" As he spoke, they saw several dignitaries climb down from the train; one of them, a Mr Huskisson who was an MP for Liverpool, walked to the Prime Minister's carriage and shook hands with him. It was well-known that the two men had argued, and Huskisson apparently wished to make his peace with the Duke.

At this moment there was a shout from many onlookers to warn the men on the trackside of an approaching train. Alfred and Lilly looked on in horror as they saw the dignitaries scatter, some climbing back into their train and others hurrying across the tracks and out of the way.

Mr Huskisson, however, seemed to be unable to make up his mind and finally grabbed the door of the Prime Minister's carriage to help himself up. But the door swung open, placing the unfortunate man right in the path of the oncoming train. The driver frantically tried to slow his engine – it was the *Rocket* itself – but it knocked Huskisson down and ran over his leg. There were cries of shock and distress and nearby spectators rushed to assist the injured man. Lilly was in tears as she watched.

"Why the 'ell didn't 'e get out o' the way?" gasped Alfred. "'E 'ad enough time! Come on, Lil; we're goin' 'ome!" He took Lilly's hand and they made their way slowly away from the crowd to find a carriage back home to Liverpool. They read in the next morning's paper that the MP had died from his injuries.

This was the country's first dramatic lesson that railways could be dangerous. Alas, it was not to be the last.

Not everyone accepted the new systems; many felt they were noisy and smelly and frightened the livestock, yet soon business interests overcame much local objection, and small, local railways began to appear all over the country, spurred on by the remarkable achievement of the railway between Liverpool and Manchester. Other towns began to consider the feasibility of short railway links, which could transport large numbers of people or goods at speeds which neither stagecoaches nor canals could match over short distance. Engineering companies began to turn to constructing railway locomotives in increasing numbers, with varying degrees of success. They were discovering that making safe railway engines was not as straightforward as it had been for stationary engines. The higher pressures required needed improved safety release valves; this discovery came at some cost, as exploding boilers not only destroyed the engines but also maimed or killed those in the vicinity. Further, these men were often experienced enginemen and therefore harder to replace.

But it was not only the industry that needed to learn about this new transport system which offered so much. The public also had to find out the hard way that railways could be dangerous.

2 - A Wider Wisdom
(Sept 1833)

In a spacious and well-appointed room above a Truro inn, three men were gathered over their drinks. Two were enjoying whiskies and the third was supping a cider. From their apparel, it was clear the whisky drinkers were men of substance, whereas their companion was less expensively dressed but apparently perfectly comfortable among his elders and betters.

"This new railway between Liverpool and Manchester is making a great deal of money for its investors, Joseph," remarked Theodor Flint, the taller of the two businessmen, "and not only that: it's also doing wonders for the businesses in both cities. My business colleague here–" he pointed to the shorter, silent man – "and I are looking for information at the request of some businessmen of Bristol who propose building a railway as well."

"Oh aye?" said Joseph, "an' where to? Gloucester, or er – Plymouth, p'raps?" This latter city mentioned with a mocking laugh. His West Country accent showed in his longer vowels.

"London."

Joseph sat up in wonder. "Lunnon? Lunnon? Liverpool to Manchester, sirs, be forty mile; Bristol to Lunnon be more'n a 'undred!"

"We are well aware of that, Joseph," continued Flint. "Now you're a clerk in an engineering company here in Cornwall: we are tasked with seeking the name of an engineer who might be interested in working with us. To be honest, we were to ask Mr Trevithick, but we hear with sadness he has very recently passed away. However, you worked under him for a while. Did he mention any person of some eminence? Do not tell us about Mr George Stephenson or his son; both are already far too committed, we understand."

Joseph scratched his head. "Ar, he once tol' me about a Fraag–" Joseph stopped and corrected himself – "er, a Frenchie—"

"A Frenchman?" interrupted Flint doubtfully.

"Aye, a Mongseer Brunel. 'E said the man's son was also an engineer with some ability. You could try 'im."

"Isn't he the son of the man who tried to build the tunnel under the Thames?"

"Aye he waas, but he resigned because his chief caused too many problems. Trevithick said he was talented."

The two businessmen were relieved that Joseph's Cornish accent was not strong; they had needed him to interpret the barman's language, which had totally defeated them.

Flint looked at his taciturn partner. "This Brunel or his son might be in want of employment, d'you think?"

His partner responded with a brief nod. "We can but ask."

Both businessmen rose and Flint put his hand into his pocket, removed a guinea coin, and handed it to Joseph. "You have our thanks!" They left the inn.

Joseph sat with a smile on his face as he heard their coachman whip up the horses and the carriage leave on the main road to Bristol. He flicked the guinea happily into the air and neatly caught it. *If they get young Brunel, they doan know what they're in for!* he chuckled to himself. *The young feller knows what he wants and knows 'ow to get it. This railway they want to build will turn out to be something very different and special if young Brunel is involved! There'll be a cuckoo in the nest o' this 'ere rail road bisnis!*

***

Smithers, the young mapping assistant, was examining the map Brunel had left in his office with his superior, who was a cartographer.

"What had Mr Brunel planned here, sir?" asked Smithers, pointing to a spot.

"That, young fellow, is the highest point between our two cities. We may need a heavier engine to bring the trains up the gradients; that is to say, either from London or Bristol to Swindon, and then lighter engines to take them downhill again. Swindon village would be where we may change engines and crews."

"I see, sir." Smithers was impressed at the thought which had gone into such detail; indeed, he had already discovered that Mr Brunel very rarely did anything without considerable forethought and planning. He was additionally a very hard worker, often working twenty hours a day.

It is sometimes difficult to find the man each morning when I come on duty; he is many miles away on horseback somewhere, leaving me only a brief note as to what I am to do, mused the young assistant. *I will either have to leave his employ or learn from him. Perhaps the latter would be the wiser course in the long run!*

One morning some months later, the two men were working near Chippenham, surveying part of the route, when the young assistant noticed something which struck him as odd. The route itself had been decided but one of the details seemed unusual: the width for a railway appeared to be excessive. This was strange since Brunel was always careful about the details. The assistant checked and compared their plan for the day against others; they showed the same width throughout the route. He decided to tackle the subject directly. "Sir, I notice we are allowing a larger gap than I would have deemed needful for a railway with two sets of rails. What is the reason for this?"

"How wide would you suggest for our gauge then?" replied his chief with an amused expression on his face.

"Er, at a width of just under five foot, I would think."

"Why less than five foot?"

"But that's what the Stockton and Darlington and the Liverpool and Manch—"

"Correct. So why did they choose that gauge?"

"Stephenson chose it."

"Yes, but why?"

"I think it was the gauge of a nearby colliery railroad for the chaldrons."

"I believe that is what he said. But we are not hauling chaldrons of coal, are we? We are building a railway for people, merchandise and heavier loads, are we not?"

"Certainly, sir."

"And would you suppose a gauge of less than five feet to be

satisfactory for such a purpose? Would that not limit our potential? Would we not do better by putting a wider distance between the rails?"

"Mmm, I had not thought of that."

His chief nodded. "Nor, I suspect, had the Stephensons. I believe they took the simpler way and copied what already existed among the coal mining railways. The Stephensons were concentrating on improving their engines and they did this very well, but did they ask themselves whether their rail gauge would effectively serve a far more diverse purpose?"

"But sir, their railways generally function with satisfaction!"

"Certainly, they do, and most others agree. But if they can build fine engines for a gauge of less than five foot, imagine what they could build for a wider gauge, to carry much greater loads! Would that not enhance their profits?"

The assistant scratched his head. "Perhaps, sir," he replied doubtfully, then added more positively, "Yes; yes, I can see that."

"Did you know that some other railways are planning to build with different gauges?"

The assistant's eyes open wide. "Is that so, sir?"

"Some Scottish railways are proposing four-foot-six; the London and Blackwall Railway plans to build their railway with a gauge of five feet; and the Ulster Railway is preparing to build at a gauge of six-foot-two."

"And you, sir?"

His chief smiled. "I'll tell you when Mr Brunel has decided. You will have observed that he left enough space for a later decision on the matter?"

"Yes, sir. I did see that, which is why I enquired." Again, the young man was impressed with Mr Brunel, who had prepared for any possible development and could make up his mind when it suited. What his chief did not tell his young companion was that Brunel had already made his mind up that a gauge of seven feet would give his Great Western Railway a serious advantage over most others.

***

The short train from Maidenhead crawled slowly out of Ealing with its crew working hard to try and catch up the twenty minutes they had already lost.

"She's just not pulling, Henry, and I am helpless to do much about it!" Driver Bertram Pritchard was frustrated; he had come from a northern railway company and was an experienced driver. "These big Great Western engines don't seem to be reliable. They're often failing on the road, and we get the blame."

"I've been shovelling as hard as I can, Mr Pritchard." The young fireman was anxious about his job; it was well paid compared to most others, and he didn't want to lose it.

"You don't have to worry about that, Herb; I know you do your best. I've had firemen up north who had no notion of firing. You may be young still, but you've got promise, I can tell."

Herbert Jones was relieved to hear this; he was only nineteen, and very interested in the new railways. His older cousin drove a stagecoach and boasted that the new-fangled railways would not last.

"You've got to get used to horses, Herbie!" he would say. "There's no future in these railways."

"The horses I like are made of iron!" Herbert had countered, but his cousin had just laughed. Herbert shook his head at the thought. *When will Alfred see his error?* he wondered as he picked up the shovel again and turned to the tender.

"Why is our engine called *Neptune*, Mr Pritchard?" he asked.

"That's what the builders called it; all our engines have names," his driver replied. "Where I come from, some railways just number their engines. But I would like to pitch *Neptune* into the sea where I believe she belongs," he grumbled.

However, they managed to persuade the engine to drag the train into Paddington, albeit fifty-two minutes late.

As they did so, the locomotive maintenance engineer, Daniel Gooch, looked on. He saw with annoyance that *Neptune* was obviously not steaming well, and there was a grinding noise from somewhere under the boiler. This engine could no longer be used until it had been taken in for examination and repair. *Neptune* was definitely not one of their better engines.

At the same time in Southall, another train – with *Bacchus* at the head – laboured slowly into the station, steam emanating from underneath the boiler, and halted. The annoyed stationmaster was waiting on the platform. "You are twenty-seven minutes late, Driver! What is the cause of this delay?"

"I do not know, sir. She simply will not pull, and there is something seriously amiss. I suspect the valve but am unable to discover the exact cause. Unless you have a spare engine, I doubt we will get her to Paddington."

The stationmaster frowned; "*Aeolus* is waiting here to take the following train in. I shall have to use her to help you to Paddington." He walked over to where Driver Nicholas Bates was waiting on the footplate of *Aeolus* with his fireman, Leonard Wetherby, getting ready to take the following train to Paddington ninety minutes later.

"I know you are waiting to take the later train, Driver, but I am directing you to take over *Bacchus*'. We must get the passengers to Paddington at all costs. They are already almost thirty minutes late. I want you to inform Paddington that they must send us another engine for your intended train."

Driver Bates sighed, "Yes, sir. Er – what about *Bacchus*?"

"You will attach to the front of her and take her with you."

"But we may not manage the train and the engine together, sir."

"You will do your very best, Driver. I have no other choice. I cannot repair her here; she'll have to go the workshop in West Drayton, so you will have to take her as well. There is no other way I can get her to the works."

"Sir." Nicholas lifted his hat in respect and turned to his fireman. "Check the coal level, Len; we're taking the whole train with the failing *Bacchus*."

The run would be a sore trial for both men. *Aeolus* herself was in reasonable condition, and they had been looking forward to a steady run, but with the weight of the train in addition to the failed engine, this duty was going to be a very different matter. Bates went over to speak to *Bacchus*' driver, to see whether he could use their engine to assist; the latter agreed that he would but doubted that it would help much. He and his fireman had been struggling just to keep her going, but they would do what they could.

"They're going to try and assist, but we mustn't expect too much," Driver Bates told his mate.

"No surprise there, then," remarked Len drily, "You c'd 'ear that as they came in, even if you couldn't see 'em."

As they slowly left Southall, any hope they might have had in making up any lost time was soon dashed. *Aeolus* was able to move the whole train, but the extra weight of *Bacchus* was telling, and any thought of speed was out of the question. They struggled to maintain about twenty miles per hour in the hope of at least not losing more time but at Hanwell *Bacchus* expelled a sudden burst of steam and ceased to pull, thus abandoning any attempt at help and simply becoming a dead weight to be carried along. By Ealing their speed had reduced to less than 15 mph.

"At least they ain't actin' as a brake," commented Len, "we're still movin' forward." Driver Bates made no reply.

They crept painfully into Paddington and Driver Bates applied the brake. The train pulled up at the platform. "Thank the Lord we finally got here, Len. I didn't think we'd make it."

Once the carriages were withdrawn, they backed, pushing the failing *Bacchus* in front of them, into the sidings leading to the engine house. But this was as far as they got because another engine was standing on the same track. Two fellow drivers were standing next to it, talking, and Bates could see a third engine beyond. He recognised his friend, Harry Burke.

"What's all this, Harry?" he enquired. "I've got a faulty engine; she won't pull again. We were over seventy minutes late in with a Maidenhead train."

"Ye'll have to wait your turn, Nick. We've got two more faulty engines 'ere an' all. They're waiting to be seen by Mr Gooch."

Bates walked a little further to see which engines Harry was talking about. "Ah, yes," he nodded. "I've driven both last week and they were not much of an improvement on this machine," he said, jerking his thumb back at *Bacchus*.

The other driver Bates did not know well; he was a Yorkshireman who had only recently been appointed.

"Aye, well my engine's fine if yer want ter boil yer mug o' tea," he assured them both, "but if ye're wantin' ter tek yer passengers anywhere, ye're wastin' yer time!"

As they were talking, a senior assistant came over and shook his head sadly. "More engines to be looked at? Mr Gooch won't be pleased."

"Aye, well we wasn't pleased either, to be given such engines!" said the Yorkshireman. "I've driven better engines in Newcastle!"

"Don't blame young Mr Gooch," stated the assistant firmly. "He didn't design them. He does his best with what we've got."

This didn't satisfy the Yorkshireman. "The passengers are blamin' us. They say we don't know 'ow ter drive!"

"Then, Driver Hardcastle, I'd advise you to take your complaint to Mr Brunel." The irritated assistant turned and walked away but stopped and turned back. "But before you do, ask around if other companies are looking for drivers; Mr Brunel doesn't like complaints!" He stalked off.

No driver was prepared to see Brunel and complain; they all wanted to keep their jobs.

As it chanced, Gooch himself had watched the arrival with *Aeolus* pulling *Bacchus*.

"How can we keep our timetable with our engines constantly failing like this?" he demanded of a nearby worker. "People are beginning to lose their trust in us!"

He felt that the engines Brunel had ordered were, in the main, unsatisfactory; he knew that Brunel had ignored the advice given to him by the manufacturers, some of whom had expressed doubt as to details in his designs.

"I expect it is only a minor failing, sir. I have full confidence that you can correct the problem." The worker dutifully expressed his faith in the young engineer. Gooch had equal confidence that he could not.

Complaints from passengers continued to mount until the unreliability of the majority of engines began to seriously worry the directors, and action was taken. They ordered a full investigation and asked Gooch to suggest improvements. Brunel was unimpressed but finally agreed, and new designs were sent to the builders. When Gooch's engines arrived, they immediately proved superior, and much less prone to failure, which led gradually to the older engines being either modified or put to one side, and to far fewer passenger complaints.

On a platform at Reading, two passengers awaiting the next up train watched as its engine arrived slowly in front of them.

"Look, sir, at the bulk of this engine spread across the seven feet! I sometimes travel on one of the northern railways with their narrower gauge and in my view this wider gauge gives a smoother ride."

His companion shook his head. "But we have to change trains when we want to travel north, do we not? I do not see the wider gauge as an advantage."

"But my dear sir, look at the loads the Great Western gauge allows; and there is a further advantage, you may not have realised, do you see?"

"Oh? Pray what would that be?"

"Tell me this: why did that unfortunate MP die on the railway near Liverpool seven years back?"

"He was run over by a train!"

"Indeed he was, but why was he run over?"

"Because he was standing between the rails, of course!"

"Yet on this railway, since he was less than seven foot tall, he could have laid himself down between the rails, and the train would have run over him without harming a hair on his head!"

3 - The Western Makes its Mark
(Sept 1841)

One day in 1841, a train from Reading arrived in Paddington, hauled by an engine designed by Mr Gooch and built by Sharp, Roberts & Co of Manchester. It bore the name *Panther* along the footplate and had huge driving wheels seven feet in diameter, a vast haycock domed firebox, a large boiler, and a tall chimney. Its run to Reading and back had been on time in both directions. The run had been fast and comfortable with no difficulties for the enginemen. They were delighted.

"I wonder whether this is the forerunner of good, new engines," remarked Driver Arnold Melling as he pulled the locomotive brake on. "She's given us a fine run for a change."

"I'd make them welcome at any rate," responded Richard Stillman, his fireman, leaning forward to shut the firebox doors. "I'm thinking of leaving for another railway with more trustworthy engines; having passengers abusing us and telling us we can't drive is beginning to anger me." He slammed the fire doors shut and wiped his hands on his trousers then climbed down to the track and uncoupled their engine from its carriages in order for another engine at the other end to draw them away for cleaning. "Two more months of poor engines and I will be looking up to the Geordies, or the London and Southampton Railway."

"Well then," replied Driver Melling, "we must look to the future with optimism and hope that the newer engines will ease our tribulations. Then we can keep you."

Over the subsequent years, the driver's optimism appeared to be well-founded; Mr Gooch's engines proved their reliability, and passenger numbers began to swell. The company's reputation received a further unanticipated boost when the young Queen Victoria, with Albert her consort, decided to return to London by means of the Great Western Railway. This decision caused some concern in the engine house at Paddington, and a senior foreman called a meeting of recent drivers of their engines.

One driver held his hand up, "I drove *Falcon* last week, sir, and it ran very well from Reading."

"And I had *Jupiter*, sir, from Oxford yesterday. She took only seventy-three minutes – and with seven loaded carriages," another claimed.

Driver Henderson put his hand up. The foreman looked at him. "Yes?"

"'Tes my opinion, sir," Henderson spoke slowly and with a measured tone, "that the Fenton engines are the most trustworthy."

The foreman nodded; that reflected his own view. He turned to his junior foreman. "Take *Phlegethon* and *Ixion* out of service for examination. We'll pick the better of the two and keep the other in case she is needed."

Phlegethon was the final choice, and she was given a fresh coat of paint and fuelled with choice lumps of coal.

On the Saturday, the engine, smartly turned out, and with the Queen's special carriage in the train, was waiting at Slough Station as the royal party arrived from Windsor and embarked. The Queen's carriage had been specially built in Swindon a year or two earlier, in the hope that she would want to use it to travel between London and Windsor Castle. Her trip to Paddington from Slough proved highly satisfactory and she expressed great pleasure. She did, however, insist that the speed should not exceed thirty miles per hour, and that the train should stop whenever she needed to eat a meal.

The Queen remarked on how comfortable, smooth and rapid the trip was on the Great Western Railway in contrast to the jolting which occurred on most roads in a horse-drawn carriage. Her comments were well publicised in the newspapers of the day and did much to further the already improving reputation of the GWR.

Yet further publicity was to prove another boost to the company's reputation, although the Great Western was this time only an accessory rather than fully deserving of the praise. A railway telegraph had been used by the Slough police to warn London's constabulary that a man they wanted was on a London train and, as a result, the murderer had been caught eighteen miles away in London, less than twelve hours after his crime in Slough. The arrest made headlines in all the newspapers of the time and the GWR rejoiced over their good fortune.

Yet on another topic altogether, the company benefitted considerably. It was a wet and foggy morning as a team of platelayers were preparing to set out and lay another stretch of Brunel's track. They were led by Jonathon Hayter, the foreman in charge. Hayter was a stickler for accuracy and was thus disliked intensely by many of his men. Jack Sawyer was one of them and as he swung his hammer to drive a marking stake into the earth, muttered to his mate Bertie Frome, "I'd give 'arf me pay for a week ter drive this 'ere stake inter 'Ayter's 'ead!"

"'E's on'y doin' 'is dooty, Jack!" said Bertie.

"Yeh, but why's 'e so blasted fiddly? An inch out an' 'e's at yer froat!"

"'E's gotter foller 'is orders, like."

"Lissen Bertie: 'ow many inches in seven foot?"

Bertie's eyebrows shot up. "'Ow the 'ell should I know?"

"Count 'em!"

"Er – must be, er – ninety?" Bertie was no mathematician.

"It's eighty-four, yer useless devil!"

"Yeah, so?"

"One inch is less'n one percent; an' bloody 'Ayter's fussin' about one percent!" But as Jack spoke, he felt a sudden thump against the side of his head, and he fell over on his face. He got up quickly with his fists raised to punch out whoever had hit him but stopped suddenly when he saw Mr Hayter in front of him.

"How much do we pay you, Sawyer, you idle fool?"

Jack thought he had lost his job through his careless talk. "I'm sorry, Mr Hayter, I was only—"

"What would you say if there were only ninepence and three farthings instead of tenpence in your pay packet?"

"Er, I'd ask why, sir, t'wouldn't be right."

"No, it wouldn't be. That's why I'm complaining when you don't do what we pay you to do! Now do your duty properly, or I'll find someone else who will!"

"Yessir!"

Hayter stalked away with a satisfied glint in his eye: he'd enjoyed hitting Sawyer. The man was a lazy shirker who was constantly complaining, and the next time the man shirked, he would sack him.

Jack watched Hayter walk off then he turned back to Bert Frome. "I worked fer the London and Birmingham for six months, Bertie, an' they lay their track twice as fast we do 'ere."

"Yeah, but they on'y work ter four-foot-eight," countered his friend. "'S not the same is it?"

"Course it's the same! The rails is on'y further apart!"

"But we 'ave ter set in these 'ere piles an' all."

Jack snorted in disgust, "That's just so that their mates sellin' them piles make more money!"

"Yer mean we don't need 'em?"

"Course we don't! The trains on the L & B run orlright without failin' all the time like ours do. It's all this fuss about 'arf an inch 'ere, and two inches there. Even bloody Shakespeare knew better!" Sawyer added with a grin.

"Shakespeare? The cove wot wrote the plays?"

"Aye. 'E wrote a play about it. He called it 'A lot o' bollocks about nowt'."

"'E did not!" Bertie laughed. "A lot o' bollocks is wot you're talkin'!"

"Straight, 'e did. It was about three 'undred year ago."

But Hayter could be seen approaching again and both men grabbed their tools quickly and set to work. Bert stopped as the boss walked past and called to him. "Mr Hayter, sir; you're a man with edicashun. Did Mr Shakespeare write a play about someone workin' 'ard and gettin' nowhere?"

Hayter was both surprised and pleased to hear the question; he had not supposed that Frome had an enquiring mind.

"Something like that, Frome, yes. The play was called 'Much ado about nothing'. I'm surprised you asked about that. Can you read?" Workers in his experience were rarely able to read much.

"Err – no, sir. Jack Sawyer 'ere mentioned it, an' I wondered if 'e was pullin' me leg."

"No, he wasn't. He's quite right." And Hayter strode on. *Navvies actually thinking? What's the world coming to?*

"Yer didn't believe me, Bertie!" said Sawyer with a grin, "Shows 'ow daft y'are."

"Not me, Jack. It's you wot's daft. You spend 'arf yer time complainin' an' gettin' nowhere!"

***

The train from Reading drew slowly into Paddington and came to a gentle stop at the block. Passengers began to disembark and move along the platform to the waiting carriages or friends, or simply to walk out towards their own destinations.

One gentleman stopped next to the engine and called to the enginemen.

"Thank you, sirs," he spoke slowly. "That was the best run I have had so far with your railway. I often need to travel up to the capital, and in previous trips we have often been rather late, with unanticipated stops due to engine failures. This time everything has accorded with your published timetable. Have you acquired new engines, or is there some other explanation?"

Driver Williams leaned over to the boiler and patted it. "It's our newer engines, sir. They are more reliable, and we are phasing our older ones out as soon as these newer engines are bought."

"I am very glad to hear that, sir. I shall travel with the Great Western Railway with more confidence now." He doffed his top hat and departed with a pleased smile on his face.

"Looks like we've got a satisfied passenger there, Bill," Driver Williams remarked to his mate.

"Aye, Mr Williams, we could do with more of 'em," muttered his mate before climbing down to the track to uncouple their engine. Bill Mathieson was of a more pessimistic nature, and his view was confirmed by their next duty. They found themselves in charge of an older engine, *Bacchus*, on a train to Maidenhead.

Williams sighed as he saw it. "You are right, Bill," he said, "we do need more of the better engines. *Bacchus* is a poor runner. I had her two weeks ago and she is not what we want on a passenger train. We might be late in Maidenhead this afternoon."

Luckily, the train was not a heavy one. Nevertheless, they

struggled for power and were already twenty minutes behind time in Slough. When starting, for a few moments it was a touch and go whether Williams could persuade the engine to move, but finally he did. The next stretch to Maidenhead did not 'accord with the published timetable', as the previous passenger had elegantly expressed it. *Bacchus* showed serious reluctance to move more than about fifteen miles per hour.

Driver Williams shook his head in anger. "We're going to be very late again, Bill."

"We're doing our best, Mr Williams," grunted Bill, shovelling hard.

"Of course we are," growled Williams, "but the passengers will all complain again anyway. They'll think we can't drive."

"They're right with this engine." Bill paused in shovelling while he took a bright red cloth from his pocket and mopped his face. "It's a pity we can't use my sweat to put water in this boiler: it's demanding enough from me."

As if the engine had heard the enginemen, and to the shock of both, it began to increase its efforts and speed. Williams stared at the smoke from the chimney, which had begun to turn paler.

"Bill, did you notice anything odd about the coal as you shovelled it in?"

"Not really, but some of the lumps from the back of the tender seem a bit glossier. Why?"

"I'm wondering whether the coal has anything to do with our problem today."

"Mmm." Bill didn't appear to be convinced. "Stoker Jeffries yesterday complained about *Bacchus* to me; he said she wouldn't pull for his driver either. He also said that Jeffries had overheard the chief grumbling to his assistant that some their early engines were freaks!"

"I've been driving with the Great Western since 1838, and I agree!" commented Williams. He decided that further discussion was useless; the new engines would solve their problems in time. Arriving in Maidenhead forty minutes late, the two enginemen busied themselves on the footplate as far from the platform as possible, thus making it more difficult to hear the complaints expressed loudly from their passengers leaving the station.

On their return to Paddington their engine was *Cyclops*, one of Mr Gooch's new engines, and, as if to compensate for their poor down run, their up run with a moderately heavy load was faultless; there was no hesitation from the engine and Bill stoked her with less coal than *Bacchus* had required. The run gave them both the chance to savour the relative smoothness of their ride; riding in *Cyclops* felt distinctly more like gliding along the track.

In Paddington, as they drew to a stop Driver Williams smiled at his fireman. "We won't be hearing any complaints this time, Bill!"

Two days later in the engine house, they saw that *Bacchus* had been towed onto a siding with its fire out and missing its tender; some of its instruments had been removed and lay on the track next to it.

"I think *Bacchus* has made her final run, Mr Williams," Bill remarked. "She won't be plaguing us again!"

"Shame, really," the driver countered. "She's only five years old."

"Well, we'll see what we get today," replied Bill as they walked together to their duty.

They were in luck; it was *Hecate*, another of Mr Gooch's new engines.

Williams grinned at his mate, "Do you know who *Hecate* was?"

"No, Mr Williams, who?"

"She was the goddess of witchcraft!"

"That doesn't bode well for our run today!"

But Bill was mistaken, for the day's duty was not troubled. They took their train to Swindon and return, keeping to their timetable within a minute both ways. Both men were tired but relieved as they pulled up in Paddington at the end of their shift.

A passenger stopped by as Bill was uncoupling *Hecate* from its carriages, calling to Driver Williams. "My congratulations, Driver, an excellent trip from Swindon!"

"Thank you, sir. We do our best."

"Do you know, I sometimes have to travel by train to Manchester, and the journey there, by the London and Birmingham and then the Grand Junction, is nowhere near as pleasant. It is not that their locomotive engines break down at all; it is rather that their carriages are narrow and cramped compared to yours. Further, sir, the ride itself in your company's carriages, with no greater velocity, is done in greater comfort. Is this due to your greater distance between the rails, or is it the excellence of your driving?"

Driver Williams was naturally delighted to hear this and responded with pleasure. "Why, sir, I am sure that our drivers are no less capable. Indeed, I have driven myself with the London and Birmingham and am not aware of any difference in ability between us. No, sir, I am persuaded that our trackwork, admittedly inconvenient when the traveller changes to other companies, is superior in both quality and design, and hence gives a smoother ride."

The gentleman nodded as if considering, then said, "I believe you are quite correct, and it remains for me to thank you and your companion for the ride." He touched his hand to his hat and departed.

By this time Bill had climbed back into the cab. "What did that toff say, Mr Williams?"

"He congratulated us for the smooth ride."

"Man of some intelligence then," commented Bill.

But two of the company's senior shareholders on the same journey expressed contrasting views regarding the speed with which the train was run.

"I fear, Dr Fisher," one shivered, speaking to his companion, "that our company's problems have not ceased, they have merely changed their form."

"How so?" enquired his neighbour in surprise. "This day has been most successful: we have attained a great velocity, and Mr Gooch's engine has proved its worth, surely?"

"We shall find ourselves in a court of law, sir, when we are accused of killing our passengers with such rapidity, which as you know, can shake a man's skull and make him incapable for further cogitation, leading to his death!"

"You are a medical man, sir?" queried Dr Fisher.

"Of course not; as you well know, being in a similar business to myself."

"Then I fail to see how you can argue on such an issue beyond your field of expertise?"

"You are of course correct, sir. Yet I, like any sensible man, consult those who are experts in their field. It is clear to me that you will not have read of Doctor – now I have forgot the man's name – let us call him 'Smith' for the sake of dispute. The good doctor maintains that the human brain cannot function with satisfaction if the body travels regularly at a greater velocity than thirty miles in an hour. We have travelled at almost twice that, sir!"

"I see, sir." The good doctor nodded politely, lifted his hat and left, muttering a further indistinct word as he did so.

The first man was astounded and spluttered in fury. "Did you call me an imbecile, sir?" he demanded of the other's retreating back. "For that, I demand satisfaction!"

The doctor stopped instantly, turned and stared. "Satisfaction? Come, man! I was merely trying to remove a piece of meat stuck in my tooth! Has perhaps the rapidity of the journey perhaps affected your ability to cogitate?" He moved off again as the first man fumed in helpless outrage.

On the platform opposite, a down Maidenhead train was waiting with Driver Harwood and his fireman Simon watching the arrival of the Reading train.

"Remember what I was telling you recently, Simon? That's *Hecate*, one of Mr Gooch's engines come from the Reading direction on time and ready to do it all again!" Harwood smiled cheerfully. "Looks like we're now getting some better engines."

"What about our engine, Mr Harwood? Is *Cerberus* one of the Gooch engines?"

"It is, Simon, and we're driving it!"

"Slough, here we come!" chortled Simon.

They made their journey there and back on time.

4 - It Pays to Watch the Time
(March 1852)

Albert Young, the driver of the train from Birkenhead to Chester, was pleased. He was allotted engine No. 3 with the name of *Touchstone*. This was an unusual engine in that it had two large steam domes, one near the chimney and the other over the firebox. It therefore had the advantage, in Driver Young's eyes, that it drew attention to itself and hence also to its driver, who paid much attention to his appearance. A short man, he always wore a tall top hat to increase his apparent size, and he was especially happy when he was teamed with fireman Henry Appleby. Appleby was of average height but with his hat Driver Young seemed to observers to be the taller of the two men. It also helped, of course, that Albert had devised a small, ingenious wooden platform to stand on. It folded up when he carried it and appeared to add two inches to his stature.

It had puzzled Henry. "If I may be permitted to ask, Mr Young, why do you bear that strange board with you?"

"This, my boy?" asked his driver, pointing to the wooden platform he was standing on. "Why, 'tis for my feet. I have weak feet, do you see, and they need frequent massage by the slats I have built into the board."

"Thank you, sir; that has eased my curiosity." Henry glanced at Albert's hat and then his little board. Surely, wondered Henry, the shaking of the engine's footplate would provide massage enough! Then another reason occurred to him. *Ah! His board and hat together must add a minimum of ten inches to the little man's height! And since I must bend to fill the firebox, he will often appear to be the greater man on the engine!*

Henry was chuckling to himself at this realisation, and they were nearing the end of their run only a few miles north of Chester when he looked ahead and, startled, called to his driver, who was busy adjusting his hat for the best angle at which to impress the passengers at Chester Station.

"Cows on the line ahead, Mr Young!"

"What?" Driver Young stared ahead and saw them. "That thrice-damned farmer!" he shouted to his fireman. "Why can't they keep their stock off our tracks?" He urgently tried to bear down on the regulator to slow the train, and Henry leaned as hard as he could on the tender brake, but it was clear the train was not going to stop in time to avoid at least injuring, if not killing, a cow or two. However, in the last seconds a dog flashed across the tracks, barking frantically at the cattle, which swung away in panic, the engine speeding only inches past the hindmost, bellowing, cow.

"Praise the Lord!" muttered Albert Young. "When I think of all the questions and reports I'd have to write..." He tailed off and then glanced at his grinning fireman. "Did ye grab enough of that tail for a bit o' cowtail soup fer yer missus, Henry?"

"Aye, Mr Young, I did an' all." The fireman held up the bleeding tail remnant he had grabbed off the unfortunate cow as they passed the cattle. "We'd rather 'ave oxtail, but this'll do nicely. Me missus does a tasty soup."

"Lucky lad!" said the driver. "But the railway companies are still too slow at learning to fence off their land from their neighbours. Fifteen years ago, it was different! We often had cows and sheep on the line making us late and even causing accidents." The train was now picking up speed again. "We sometimes enjoyed a bit of beef or mutton, so it wasn't always bad news!"

As he spoke, Albert noticed that they were approaching the little station at Mollington and he slowed the train, bringing it gently to a halt. There were a few ladies waiting there to board for their shopping in the city.

After three more miles, they arrived at the city station and Henry climbed down to uncouple from their coaches. They were off duty now and the Shrewsbury and Chester Railway engine was waiting to couple up and take the train further south.

In the city itself, Driver Josiah Frode paused as he waited for the points to switch over and allow him to move to the station, where he was to couple up to take the passenger train from

Birkenhead south to Shrewsbury; the carriages had already arrived from Birkenhead and were waiting on the platform for them. But as he moved over towards the platform, he felt uneasy: something about the engine was not right. He glanced down the boiler lagging and noticed a slight shimmer on one side. He then looked at the safety valve.

"God in his heaven!" he muttered. "Some idiot has tightened the safety valve!" It was not unknown for drivers to try this when an engine was reluctant to pull. Tightening the safety valve expanded the boiler pressure and gave more power. It also increased the risk of a boiler explosion, and was strictly banned. Yet the blame could not fairly be placed entirely at the hands of the drivers; on occasions trains were overloaded well beyond the capacity of the engines chosen to haul them. Boilers were not always made sufficiently strong to cope with the power generated by the water temperatures which was required to create the necessary steam pressure to haul the trains. Hitherto, boilers had not needed to produce such power; they had been designed mainly for milling machines, or to move air in and out of mines.

Josiah eased the engine well forward, past the end of the platform and away from the passengers. "George, find a fitter as fast as you can; the safety valve needs to be loosened!"

Luckily for everyone in the vicinity, a fitter with his bags of tools was nearby and when he came to see the problem he expressed himself with impressive vigour and immediately set to work to loosen the valve. The twenty-foot geyser of steam as the valve eased showed how close disaster had been. Even passengers on the platform many yards away stared in surprise; fortunately, very few realised what might have happened.

The locomotive was one of the long-boilered engines from Longridge & Co in Northumberland. The Chester and Shrewsbury Railway had bought a number of these and although they were generally satisfactory, Josiah did not like them very much. They were 2-4-0s and were mostly used as passenger engines.

His fireman, George Comerford, was busy filling the fire with coal. "You often say you don't like these engines, Mr Frode, but

I reckon they look strong and powerful with their long boilers, and with you driving they seem to keep time quite well. What don't you like about them?" George began to shovel more coal into the huge dome of the firebox.

"Now that, young George, shows your lack of experience. Have you fired one of the Sharps 2-2-2 engines yet?"

"Er, no sir, I haven't. I was supposed to last week, but they changed engines."

"Well now, when you have fired on one of those, ask me that question again if you still don't know the answer," replied his driver, smiling. If he doesn't know the answer then, Josiah thought, he'll not make an engineman. Longridge's long-boilered engines had a short wheelbase, which tended to make them unsteady at speed and uncomfortable for their crews and passengers. This made them, in Josiah's opinion, not best suited for express passenger work. Sharp's engines, he felt, ran much better.

He watched as Head Guard Henry Willis checked that all offside doors in the carriages were locked and those on the platform side were firmly shut too before he signalled that the train was ready to depart. There were still passengers who had a cavalier attitude to leaving the train whether it was moving or not. He knew who would get the blame if they lost any passengers.

Once all were safely boarded, Henry waved his flag and the train with its twenty carriages moved out of the station, gradually picking up speed. They travelled through the two tunnels and over the canal and as they neared the river Josiah had a slight concern while they crossed the water on the newly rebuilt bridge over the River Dee. There was a slight rumble that he did not like. They picked up more speed passing the Saltney works of the Shrewsbury and Chester Railway, south of the city. Originally the works of that railway, they now served the Shrewsbury and Birmingham Railway as well and even took on work for the Shrewsbury and Hereford Railway.

As the train hurried across the plain, Josiah kept a sharp eye open for the signalmen standing at the lineside to indicate whether the line ahead was clear. This wasn't easy for him because he was a short man, and the huge dome of the firebox limited his forward vision. As they passed the little stop at Balderton heading south, the engine was pulling well, and it was only minutes before Josiah began to lower the regulator to begin slowing down for a signalman holding his right hand high to indicate 'caution'. George was turning to pick up some more coal from the tender when he stopped, stunned, and stared. He saw a passenger was standing on the low outside footrest which ran the whole length of the carriage, holding tight to the handrail high up at the end of the carriage with one hand and holding onto his top hat with the other.

The man leaned forward, screaming, "Why didn't you stop this damned train at Balderton?"

"Keep tight hold of the rail, you fool!" shouted George to the passenger. "We'll be stopping soon."

Josiah overheard his fireman and, still lowering the regulator lever, turned to stare at George. "Who the hell are you shouting at?"

George pointed to the angry passenger clinging on the outside the first carriage.

"Great heavens!" exclaimed Josiah. "What an idiot! and in the first class too! We'll get the blame if the fool falls off and kills himself!"

He slowed the train right down and the fast Wolverhampton train crawled with a serious lack of dignity into Rossett Station.

When they finally came to a stop, the angry passenger dropped to the platform and stamped over to the enginemen to curse them.

Guard Willis hurried from the back of the train to enquire why the train had stopped, and saw the passenger haranguing the two enginemen. "Is there something amiss, sir?"

"Indeed there is, my man!" The passenger was exceedingly angry. "This train ran through Balderton and did not stop there. I have urgent business in the village and have missed my appointment due to the careless attitude of these men here! I am Harvey Winston, an important businessman in Chester, and I'll have you know I am a close friend of one of the Chester Assize judges."

"But this train does not stop at Balderton, sir. It is shown on the timetable as not stopping there."

"Nonsense! I have a copy of the timetable, and it clearly shows a stop at Balderton at half past nine." He pulled out the relevant document from an inside pocket and thrust it under the nose of the guard. "Look here; twenty minutes past nine from Chester, with a half-past-the-hour stop at Balderton. Clear as a bell!"

"I'm sorry, sir; you are mistaken. This train is the quarter to ten from Chester and does not normally stop until Wrexham."

By this time, the Rossett stationmaster had come out to see why the train had stopped at his station. He ignored the furious passenger and the guard, speaking sharply to Josiah. "What do you mean by stopping here, Frode? You had better have a good reason or you'll face a hefty fine!"

Josiah pointed to the passenger. "Firstly, the signalman indicated 'caution', sir; then this passenger climbed out of his carriage and was standing on the footrest, signalling us to stop. I judged it safer to stop in case he fell to his death, sir."

The stationmaster turned to Winston. "Is that correct, sir?"

"I demand to be taken back to Balderton for an appointment. You will order me a carriage! I missed the stop due to the fault of these men on the engine who did not stop!"

"This train, sir, is the quarter to ten fast train from Chester to Wolverhampton. It does not stop at Balderton, nor here at Rossett; you can see from the timetable, which," the stationmaster added pointedly, "I believe you have in your hand."

"Damn you, man!" snapped Winston. "I can read! This timetable shows the train stopping at Balderton at half past the hour." He hauled out a fine pocket watch, "It is now forty-six minutes past nine and I am late for my meeting!"

The stationmaster and Guard Willis both hauled out their watches; both showed three minutes past ten. The stationmaster showed his watch to Winston, and the guard did the same.

"What does your watch show, Driver Frode?"

Josiah took his watch out of his waistcoat and glanced at it and showed it. "Three minutes past ten, sir."

Winston was not at all mollified; he glared at the stationmaster and snapped, "I see that all you railway servants are in league to swindle your passengers! I will speak to my lawyer, and we will see what the law has to say about this!"

He turned to go, but the stationmaster stopped him. "One moment, sir. I must agree with you on one issue."

Winston paused, surprised.

"We must see what the law says," continued the stationmaster. "Now let me think: endangering the lives of enginemen and possibly even passengers, insulting railway servants, descending from a speeding train without authorisation, causing a fast train to be stopped not in accordance with the published timetable."

"Attempting to descend on a Chester and Shrewsbury Railway train," muttered George too quietly for the stationmaster to hear. Josiah coughed, turning away before the stationmaster could see his grin.

"What! What?" Winston's anger developed into a fury. "I'll see the four of you railway servants convicted in court!" He swung round to go, but the stationmaster called out, "You might need our names, sir, for your legal case. And we need your name for our defence."

"Stationmaster at Rossett and crew of the twenty-past-nine Chester to Wolverhampton!" called Winston, smirking as he left. He immediately ran into another man near the station entrance.

"Oh, pardon me, sir!" he began and then stopped in surprise and pleasure. "Mr Forsyth; well met, sir! You are just in time to assist me in preventing a blatant miscarriage of justice."

"Goodness me, Winston! Of course! How can I—"

"Your watch, Mr Forsyth, if you please. These men here," he pointed at his adversaries, "are trying to swindle me. They insist that it is past ten of the clock, and furthermore that my train is not the 9.20 to Shrewsbury, but the 9.45 to Wolverhampton. Consequently, I have missed an important engagement."

Forsyth took out his watch. "But my dear sir, it is indeed five minutes past ten, and I have just travelled on the train from Chester which departed at twenty after nine. I foolishly left my case on the train and returned to enquire how I might retrieve it."

Winston's mouth opened and shut like a goldfish in its bowl. "But, but, my watch shows—?"

"Er – please forgive the indelicacy, Winston, but did you give your watch to Jenkins last night to wind up for you?"

"Yes, of course I did—" Winston stopped. *Did I give my watch to the butler last night?* He looked at it again; it showed thirty-nine minutes past nine. "Dear me, perhaps I didn't after all. How embarrassing." But he didn't seem in any way perturbed.

"Perhaps you might save the situation and return to the men and explain with a brief apology?"

Winston stared at his friend in surprise. "Apology, Forsyth? Apology? What on earth are you thinking of? Of course, I won't apologise, they are only railway servants!"

"Then I fear, Winston, that should you pursue your court case, given the evidence of at least four railway servants and my own watch, any magistrate would be certain to find against you and award costs to the railway company. You could even face a term in prison!"

"Prison?" Winston stared at his friend in horror. "Prison?"

"A competent lawyer could claim that you had not only broken the Company's regulations, but in doing so, you endangered the lives of perhaps two hundred passengers on board the train, sir!"

"But surely—?"

"And what, pray, could you claim in your defence? A watch which, as you yourself admit, may not have been wound up the previous evening."

Winston said nothing for a moment or two, then murmured, "Your own watch, Forsyth, might have shown the same time as mine?"

Forsyth took it out again and examined it. "But it doesn't, Winston."

"You and I know it doesn't, Forsyth, but those railway servants don't know that. If you were to set it back to the time on my—" He stopped as he saw Forsyth's face turn pale.

"Are you suggesting that I perjure myself, sir?" demanded Forsyth, glaring angrily at Winston. "And join you in your possible prison sentence, all on account of a simple error on your part?"

Winston opened his mouth to deny this, but Forsyth ignored him, turned away and strode off.

"Now, Frode, get your train on the move as quickly as you can. You have lost at least eight minutes due to that idiot passenger. Have no fear of any repercussions." The stationmaster wanted as little interference to the timetable as possible. "I will endorse your report with my view that you both acted swiftly and intelligently within the Company's regulations."

"Thank you, sir, we appreciate your support." Josiah was also keen to try and make up lost time and was very pleased at the attitude of the stationmaster.

The enginemen waited until Henry had got all the passengers back into the train; several had climbed out to observe the proceedings with interest. Once he was happy that everyone was back safely in their carriages, he waved at the enginemen and climbed back into his van.

"Let us proceed then, George," said Driver Frode. "Seize your shovel and we'll see how much we can make up. It would be a feather in our caps if we were on time in Shrewsbury!"

5 - The Thin End of the Wedge
(Feb 1861)

The Midland Railway train from Birmingham slowed as it came into Gloucester Station, the doors in the carriages beginning to open as impatient passengers got ready to disembark, many of them to change into the waiting Great Western train heading for Newport or Cardiff. The change was necessary because the Midland was a narrow-gauge railway (in Great Western terms), while the GWR was still mostly broad gauge. To facilitate matters, some of the trackwork in the station area was dual gauge so that stock of both companies could use it.

Then began the usual chaos as passengers from South Wales hurried to find the best seats on the Birmingham train and tried to make their way with their luggage between the Birmingham passengers wanting to board the South Wales train.

"I wonder when the Great Western will agree to change their gauge to ours and the rest of the country's," remarked the Midland's Driver Andrew Cameron to Fireman Robert Trubshaw.

"We've got some time to wait for that, I believe. It could be years befo— Oh, good heavens! Look at that poor old lady!"

The elderly lady on the platform had been knocked over by a young man running past, and her heavy carpetbag had dropped and burst open. Several people were trying to help her retrieve its contents; two more were looking to see where the man was, and a third was pushing his way through the crowd to call a railway official or a police constable. As a result, a melee had erupted.

"How can we help here?" worried the young fireman.

"Best by doing our job," responded his driver curtly. "Now hop down and uncouple so that we can draw forward and allow the engine of this Birmingham train to couple up at the other end and get ready for the return run."

"But I—?"

"Just do what I told you," demanded Driver Cameron with

asperity. "We can best help by not getting involved and increasing the confusion."

"Yes, sir." The fireman climbed to the track. He uncoupled their locomotive and the driver eased it forward. There was a bump from the other end of the train and the carriages jerked forward slightly as the Birmingham engine buffered up to the other end. The rear carriage caught Fireman Trubshaw by surprise as he had stood next to it to watch his driver move away. The buffer beam knocked him flat onto the track. His driver saw with shock what had happened, stopped the engine immediately, and jumped down to see whether young Robert was badly hurt: the carriage had jerked forward forcefully. But, the driver was relieved to see, the fireman got up, rubbing his back and swearing furiously.

"I'll find the name of that driver when we complete our shift, you can put your money on that!" Andrew growled. "That was dangerous driving."

"Thank you, sir for that," replied Robert. "And I might have a word with him myself. I sometimes make an extra guinea in bare-knuckle boxing in our village," he explained, "when we can be sure the peelers aren't around."

His driver laughed. "Yes, but don't allow him to know who you are. A railway can be a dangerous place, lad, and he might have friends," he warned.

The fireman's face darkened. "I have friends too," he countered, "and they are boxers like me. We could always use a little extra practice."

At the nearby Great Western platform, the crowd of passengers had mostly boarded the South Wales train and the engine crew made ready to move out. At the other end of their train the engine which had brought it in was also waiting for it to leave, in order to back out into the sidings and use the turntable, ready for the return to Cardiff with a later train.

"We have to hurry with the preparation to return, Blair." Driver Jones was in a hurry.

"Why is that, Mr Jones?" Fireman Eric Blair was puzzled. "We're not due out back to Cardiff for two and a half hours."

"I've got a private matter to attend to after we've prepared the engine."

"Business?"

"Private business, so mind your Ps and Qs, young fellow," responded Jones irritably.

"Sorry, Mr Jones."

As they were speaking, the Cardiff train left, clearing the track for them to move out to the yard with the interchange sidings between the Great Western broad gauge and the Midland standard gauge. Some of the sidings were dual gauge so enginemen had to be alert, as had the shunters in the yard. Driver Jones accelerated out of the station and headed at a higher speed than was wise for the siding. This was unfortunate because it did not give the shunter enough time to reach the points to change them to the broad-gauge siding. Consequently, Driver Jones ran over the points to a standard-gauge siding, where the engine promptly derailed and tilted to one side.

Fireman Blair was holding onto a side rail on the footplate, but Jones only had hold of the regulator and lost his grip. He grabbed for a handrail but missed, lost his balance, and fell off the footplate, onto the ground. He sat up, groaning and holding his right elbow. "I think I've broken my damned arm!" he growled in pain.

Hmm, we might be late back into Cardiff, thought Blair but he wisely did not voice these thoughts. He was not comfortable with his driver, who was prone to cut corners; a very dangerous practice on a railway. By the time he had gathered his wits, other railwaymen were beginning to arrive, to shout either encouragement or useless advice, and a foreman had turned up to organise another locomotive to haul the GWR engine backwards to a point at which they could re-rail it on the broad-gauge track. His assistant was noting down the details and recording the name of the enginemen deemed responsible for the accident. They would be interviewed to decide who was responsible, and the offender would be fined for carelessness.

While the two crewmen were waiting to be questioned, Blair risked an admonishment from his evil-tempered driver.

"Would it not be easier, Mr Jones, if the Great Western were to accept the inevitable and convert to the same gauge as most other railways?"

"Blair! Have you not noticed that the Great Western has already begun to allow trains of other companies to use our tracks?" Jones snapped back, his embarrassment at his carelessness giving rise to the sharp reply.

"Sir?"

"You have eyes in your head, boy! Have you not thought of why there are stretches in which we have added a third rail to our tracks so that the inferior railway companies can run their trains over some of our system?"

It was now Fireman Blair's turn to be ashamed: he had noticed, but had not given the matter any thought. Of course! That was what it was! *Why did I not see that?* Distracted by this thought, he did not notice that their locomotive was now back on its track and, apparently without serious damage, was being steamed slowly back to its broad-gauge sidings.

The next day, Cardiff foreman Alfred Evans was sitting in his office with Driver Jones facing him. The foreman was leafing through a sheaf of papers.

"Driver Jones," he began, "you have a regrettable habit of accidents. 'May 2nd, 1856, damage to wagon; fined one shilling.' 'April 16th, 1857, broke couplings through heavy shunting; fined four shillings and sixpence.' And another, 'December 28th, 1858, knocked over a stopblock; fined three shillings.' And now this!" he stared hard at the driver. "What have you to say in your defence?"

Driver Jones was desperate. "Sir, the shunter was too slow at changing the points for me, and Fireman Blair here was having a driving practise."

Blair was shocked to the core to hear this; it was nonsense. Jones would never have allowed him to drive, and anyway the man had simply been driving too fast.

Foreman Evans glanced at Blair. "Fireman Blair?"

Blair shook his head, "I was on the tender at the time, sir. I was not aware that I was able to drive; I thought I was not permitted to."

"Curious," remarked the foreman with heavy sarcasm. "I too was under the belief that a driver is responsible for driving his engine."

Jones stayed silent in his misery.

"Driver Jones, no driver in my five years here has ever complained to me about Fireman Blair. I am quite certain he was not driving. You are hereby fined ten shillings. Further, if you ever cause another accident costing more than a shilling, you will be sacked. Further still, in trying to pass the blame onto an innocent man who could thereby face dismissal from the company, your action is contemptible. You may go. Fireman Blair, stay here, I need a word with you."

Jones left the office with eyes of fury but saying nothing. Blair felt sorry for the next fireman who had a duty with him, but he felt no sympathy for Jones; the man deserved what he had received.

"Blair," began the foreman, "this incident leaves you in a difficult position: as his regular fireman, Jones is able to give you a hard time should he desire to. If you wish to apply for a duty in another shed, I would fully understand and support your application. I have confidence that you will one day make a good driver and do not wish to hamper your progress."

"Thank you, sir, but no; I am happy here with most other drivers."

"I am glad to hear that. I will, however, move you to a different regular driver. That is all."

"Thank you again, sir." A relieved Blair left the foreman's office happier than he had been on entering.

***

Elsewhere on the system, further evidence of conversion was clear. Driver Joe Harman from Salop drew his train into Birmingham for the crew change he expected. Another crew was to take the train on to Oxford, where passengers for Paddington could change into a broad-gauge train to their destination. His ex-Shrewsbury and Birmingham engine, a 2-2-2 named *Wrekin*, would see the train through to Oxford now that the old company had been absorbed into the Great Western Railway. Driver Harman had been seeking a transfer to a broad gauge shed further to the south; he had driven broad-gauge engines several times and was impressed by the room on the footplate. *Wrekin* had a remarkably narrow cab, which did not make for comfort for the two footplatemen.

The next driver climbed up. "Any problems, Joe?"

"No, Gordon, she's running quite well. But tell me, have you heard of any driver vacancies coming at Oxford?"

"Oxford? No, why?"

"I'm thinking of changing to a shed where I can drive on the broad gauge. The cabs on these narrow engines are too small for me."

"Well, Oxford's no help; they're mostly narrow gauge now. You'd need to look further south to Paddington or the main line west."

"Are we converting everywhere, then?"

"Yes, I believe so, but it will take many years yet," Gordon explained with a distinct sadness in his voice. "I am convinced, Joe, that the Gauge Commissioners made a grievous error when they chose the narrow gauge as the realm's standard."

Joe nodded his agreement. "I'll have to look further south then."

He was fortunate and within two months was transferred to Swindon, from where he rarely had to work on the narrow-gauge tracks. Most trains to the west were still broad gauge, although there was increasing evidence of mixed gauge tracks over the next few years.

On a Swindon local soon after he was transferred, Joe had a Victoria class 2-4-0 locomotive on a 'running in' turn; this was to check whether a repair of some sort had been satisfactory. He asked his fireman, William Pearson, whether he was familiar with narrow-gauge engines.

"Not really, Mr Harman. I've fired a couple only but didn't like the small cab. You've got no room to swing a cat, let alone a shovelful of coal."

Joe nodded, "I know what you mean. That's why I transferred to the broad gauge."

His view was a very common one among broad-gauge men. But the narrow-gauge incursions continued, and by the mid 1860s the GWR had more narrow-gauge engines than broad-gauge and was not building many more broad-gauge locomotives. Nevertheless, Joe was fortunate in the sense that he spent the rest of his driving days on the broad gauge.

***

The express from Oxford was slowing down as it coasted through the four or five miles of approach to Paddington one cold January morning. Two men peered through the window of their first-class coach, examining the tracks of the sidings on either side of the main line as they passed through Ealing and Acton. The men were both Oxford dons and, although they taught in different areas, were friends. Dr John Williams lectured in Classics, whereas his good friend Dr Victor Anson taught engineering.

"I see the Great Western Railway is finally admitting defeat in its broad gauge, Victor," Dr Williams remarked, observing the relaying of some of the rails in which a third was being readied for insertion between the two outer broad gauge rails. "They seem to be bowing to common sense!"

"On the contrary, John." Dr Anson spoke with some asperity. "They are being bullied into abandoning engineering wisdom!"

"But surely it is to the advantage of the company to align itself with its neighbours to ease the transfer of passengers and freight, is it not?"

Dr Williams frowned, completely failing to comprehend his friend's viewpoint.

"I will readily concede the value of your argument there, John," countered Dr Anson. "However, engineering wisdom ought to have swayed the Gauge Commissioners against their decision regarding the gauge to be used by all new railways. In the long run, as it were, the broader gauge makes far more economic sense."

"How so?"

"This carriage, you will observe, has comfortable seating for sixty-four passengers. Now, carriages of a similar length on a narrow-gauge railway will seat forty-eight passengers. So a passenger train on the broad-gauge railways will accommodate perhaps one-third more passengers and consequently concomitant increase in efficiency and profit."

"But the costs of construction would be higher, would they not?"

Victor bowed his head in acknowledgement, "They would indeed, John, yet not as much as you might suppose. Once you have your locomotives and stock designed and proven, the construction costs would not vary much from those of the narrow gauge."

As the two gentlemen were pursuing their learned discourse in his train, Driver Timothy Harkness was on the footplate, shaking his head sadly and pointing out the workmen to Fireman Andrew Jackson. "Sad to see that, Andy," he called. "The narrow gauge is coming into Paddington after all these years!"

"True enough, Mr Harkness," Andy replied. "It's the thin end of the wedge!"

His driver gazed at him, puzzled. "The what?"

"It's a literary expression, Mr Harkness. It refers to the small start which leads to a big problem."

"Ah, yes." Harkness nodded; he didn't want to admit his lack of schooling: the Great Western laid great value on respectability, which included a sound education. He was more concerned with the performance of his Victoria class 4-4-0 engine, built in Swindon. He rather enjoyed the luxury of having a short roof over his head when driving.

In his early driving days, no such protection was offered; enginemen, like stagecoach drivers, were expected to provide their own protective clothing. Getting cold and wet or covered in snow was just part of the job; there was no point in complaining, and in any case the pay was good and there were plenty who were eager to take the job on if you didn't like it. A Great Western driver was a man of consequence in local society and was expected to uphold a certain social standing.

His fireman was an unusual lad; he had an education, and his parents had expected him to move into a clerical position which would presumably lead to work in business or teaching. To see him as a railway cleaner would have been a surprise to them, but the boy had persevered and was already a fireman. Harkness could see him as a competent driver in the not-too-distant future because the lad had talent for his work.

"Have you fired on one of the narrow-gauge engines yet, Andy?" asked Harkness.

"Not yet, Mr Harkness. But on a cold morning like this, I think it might be preferable."

Harkness was startled to hear that; nearly all the broad-gauge enginemen he knew had a low opinion of the narrow gauge. "Why is that?"

"You are never far from the fire," explained Andy simply. Harkness had no answer to that.

As they drew slowly into the station at Paddington, Harkness looked over to the other side of their platform to see a train with late passengers boarding in a hurry and porters shutting the doors. He stopped his train and pointed to the now departing train.

"See that, Andy?"

"Of course, Mr Harkness; I see a departing train. What about it?"

"Do you know where it is heading?"

Andy checked the platform number, considered for a moment and then replied, "I expect it's going to Didcot or Oxford."

Harkness gazed sadly at his fireman. "Andy, you're an intelligent and educated youngster, but you can be curiously slow at times. Look again, and at the carriages."

Andy studied the train again and frowned. "Yes, Mr Harkness, you are correct. That is a curious train; I hadn't noticed."

"Now tell me, what is curious about it?"

"The engine is a narrow-gauge engine and the carriages are a very mixed collection."

Harkness pointed to a passing porter. "Ask that porter where the train is for."

Andy climbed down and approached the porter and spoke to him. He returned to the cab very surprised. "That train is for Chester, Mr Harkness! Chester's over two hundred miles away!"

"Indeed; and from Chester its passengers can change onto the Chester and Birkenhead Railway and thus reach the Mersey and Liverpool. This means we can rival the London and North Western to Merseyside! We'll be running through trains soon!"

6 - Cornish Confusion
(May 1877)

"We're sending you out of our country for a spell, James," stated the foreman of Exeter shed with a grin.

"Out of our country, sir?" Young Cleaner James Baird saw the grin but was puzzled at what Mr Mason the foreman was telling him.

"That's right; you're going to Penzance."

"But Penzance is in Cornwall, sir!"

"Ar, that's so."

"Cornwall's in England, Mr Mason."

Alfred Mason rubbed his nose carefully. "Well now, that's what you might call debatable, lad. There's many here in Devon who think otherwise. In Cornwall too, there are plenty of Cornishmen who believe England is a foreign country; some of 'em even speak a different language."

James was astounded. "A different language, sir?"

"Cornish; but it's dying out. It's more like Welsh, and nothing like English, but don't worry: all railwaymen speak English – even Cornish railwaymen," he added with a laugh. "But you'll find they do things a bit different in some ways."

"How different, Mr Mason?"

"I'll let you find out for yourself, young James. But one thing you'll discover fairly quickly is that the goods trains can be very different from anything you've seen so far."

"How's that, sir?"

"It won't take you long to find out. Now you're to report to the shedmaster at Penzance next Monday at eight in the morning. You'll need the weekend to get there, find somewhere to live, and settle yourself in."

James grimaced without thinking.

"What's the problem?" asked his boss, noticing the grimace.

"Sorry, sir. It's not that I don't want to go – it's getting to Penzance; I haven't saved up enough to get there."

"Mmm – look, see me on Friday. I'll arrange something."
"Sir."

James said goodbye to his mates late on the Friday and reported early on Saturday morning to Mr Mason, who directed him to the goods yard to talk to the guard of a Truro goods. This train stood ready with a long 0-6-0 goods engine with the name *Liffey* curling on a plate over the centre driving wheel. It was one of a large class of engines built in Swindon for the Bristol and Exeter railway and James knew the type well, having cleaned many of them. They were not new, built some dozen years earlier, and they were gradually being withdrawn from service. He walked on towards the guard's van at the end, climbed onto the bottom step, and knocked on the door. It opened immediately and a head looked out.

"Ye're young Baird, are yer?" asked Guard Patterson peering down from his van and looking James up and down.

"Yes, sir, I am."

"An' ye're wantin' ter get ter Truro?"

"Yes, that's right. I need to get to Penzance for Monday morning."

"I'll give yer a lift ter Truro and I'll see if I c'n get yer further ter Penzance, then, young shaver. Hop up."

James climbed up with alacrity into the guard's van. "Thank you, sir." He looked around the van; it was a roomy vehicle, which was to be expected. As an Exeter cleaner, James briefly wondered what it would be like to work in a narrow-gauge vehicle, although of course he had seen plenty because the main line for a few miles north of Exeter was dual gauge; shared between the Great Western and the London and South Western railways. The GWR was broad-gauge, but the LSWR was narrow-gauge (the rest of the country called it standard gauge) and had an odd feature in that the London-bound trains of the GWR ran north through Exeter's St David's Station, while the London-bound trains of the LSWR ran south through it.

Guard Patterson proved to be an entertaining companion, but when asked what it was that might surprise James about goods trains in Cornwall, he shook his head.

"Can't think what yer shedmaster means about that," he said, frowning. "I'm on 'em nearly every day, an' they seem normal ter me. But they are a bit slow, like; the track's not as well laid in some places as it is elsewhere. P'raps that's what he's thinkin' of."

James nodded, but privately he felt that there was something else. Either the guard really didn't know what the Exeter shedmaster meant, or the guard was in on some joke or other. Well, this cleaner would keep his eyes open and see! He had been in the job long enough to know that cleaners were often the butt of jokes and tricks, although not as a rule from shedmasters. In the meantime, he would just enjoy the free ride, and hope he could get another from Truro to Penzance.

They were coming to the great Royal Albert Bridge built by Brunel at Saltash and James gazed out at its imposing entrance arch, with its proud inscription of Brunel's name in large letters: 'I K Brunel Engineer 1859'. *What a shame*, thought James, *that Brunel had been too ill to attend the opening ceremony by Prince Albert himself.* The engineer had died shortly after the opening and never got to travel over his bridge. James gazed down at the River Tamar a hundred feet below. The bridge had been designed so that great ships could sail below it; admittedly, some would have to remove their topmasts to pass under.

On reaching the Cornish side of the river, James kept his eyes carefully peeled to see what Mr Mason had been discussing so slyly, but there was nothing obvious apart from the inferior state of some stretches of track. The train slowed down occasionally, he noticed; these bad patches were clearly well known, and drivers were ready for them. The Cornwall Railway didn't have the financial resources of the Bristol and Exeter or the Great Western railways, he assumed. The high trestle bridges were spectacular and in James' eyes they looked flimsy, however they must have been stronger than they looked because they did not appear to worry Guard Patterson as he filled in his papers.

Once they reached Redruth, James was surprised to see mixed trackwork again and turned to the guard. "Mr Patterson, sir, why is there mixed gauge track here? I thought we were all broad gauge in the West Country."

"Not all, young feller. We join the Hayle Railway here, which was always narrer gauge and is an important line fer minerals and suchlike. Ye'll see plenty of vans and especially wagons fer clay an' tin an' wotnot. If ye're ter work here, ye'll likely be seein' plenty in Penzance harbour."

As they trundled slowly into Redruth yard, James saw many sections of mixed and even narrow-gauge track in the yards, with wagons of both gauges often on the same track, which puzzled him. *Why do they mix them together? They can't possibly be put into the same train: they're different gauges!* This was very confusing, and he shook his head; no doubt the matter would be cleared up when he got to Penzance. Guard Patterson didn't make any mention of the riddle and James didn't want to ask and thus show his ignorance. He was, after all, an experienced cleaner, and almost ready to take up fireman training!

Their train steamed slowly into the yard and drew to a halt. Here he saw the same mixture of tracks of different gauges but only a very few were of one gauge only. But his eyebrows shot up in shock to observe a goods train composed of vehicles of both gauges slowly arriving from the west; it pulled into a siding and the fireman climbed down to uncouple the engine, which then trundled off. Shunters were beginning to uncouple the vehicles when Guard Patterson said, "Now, young feller, it was Penzance yer wanted ter go ter, wasn't it?"

"Yes, that's right, sir." But James' eyes were still glued to the goods train.

The guard nodded. "I'll see what I c'n do fer yer, then." He walked off towards a small building fifty yards away. "Come along then," he called.

James followed him towards the building, shaking his head at what he seen. Inside was a small office with a man sitting at a desk, busy with papers. He smiled as he saw the guard. "Howdo, Albert; good to see you. Who's this young fellow you've got with you?"

"He's a cleaner from Exeter, Jerry, an' he needs ter get ter Penzance by Monday mornin' ter sign on there. 'E's bin transferred, but they 'aven't given 'im a travel warrant. Can we do summat fer 'im?"

Jerry smiled and looked James up and down. "It's your lucky day, young cleaner, you've had some experience in a goods train, haven't you?"

James paused, embarrassed. "Not really, sir, I have to say."

"Yes, you have. You've just come from Exeter in a goods train with Guard Patterson here, if I'm not mistaken?"

"Ah, well, yessir."

"Excellent, you see the guard for the Penzance goods has just reported in with a bad leg and tells me he can serve his shift, but he needs an assistant. And now I have one! It's an easy duty. Just do what he tells you: nip out and couple or uncouple from time to time. I'll put you on the books and we'll even pay you. How does that sound?"

"Thank you, sir; it sounds highly satisfactory!"

"You have thirty minutes to get yourself a mug of tea – Guard Trelawney will show you where – and then you join him on the Penzance goods."

James left the office and saw the goods waiting on the down departure siding; he walked to the guard's van and climbed in. The guard was a tall man with his leg stretched out under the little bench.

"My assistant, I imagine?"

"Yes, sir. Cleaner James Baird, transferred from Exeter shed to Penzance. I'm to assist you on my way there today."

"Good." He eyed James' bag. "Stick your bag under the bench here but get your mug out. You'll take tea with me before we leave, I expect?"

"Willingly, sir."

"Our first stop is at Camborne to offload wagons then we stop again at Gwinear Road for a Helston drop off, Hayle for the harbour traffic, and finally at St Erth for the St Ives branch. We're due in Penzance at about four-thirty, but we'll almost certainly be late. Goods traffic on this line can be slow."

James nodded. "Very good, sir." He sipped his tea.

They left soon after and the train steamed steadily out of the yard and onto the main line, where James was surprised to discover that they did not speed up as much as he expected. He sent a querying look to the guard, but he was busy with his papers. They pulled in at Camborne to deposit a set of wagons and then James found out why the goods trains were slow: the differing gauges of the wagons made marshalling them a nightmare! Shunters in Redruth had tried hard to gather wagons for each destination together but even so, uncoupling a narrow-gauge wagon from a broad-gauge wagon took time as the buffers were sometimes replaced with long beams.

James learned that so-called 'converter' wagons were used to link vehicles of different gauges to each other; these had longer beams instead of buffers so that the vehicles could buff up to each other. Couplings were not so far apart as to cause difficulty. He noticed in mixed gauge track, too, that their freight train – never fast – slowed down at the approach to stations because the narrow-gauge track eased over to use the inside rail for the common rail along the platforms; this was in order to align coaches of both broad- and narrow-gauge passenger trains to use the same platform face.

In the yards the driver had to watch that the siding he was directed into was mixed gauge; some were not. Shunters occasionally made mistakes, directing a mixed train into a single-gauge siding. When this happened, it was followed by loud, insulting language in all directions and burdensome form-filling. Nevertheless, the shunting was successfully completed, and they could move on to Gwinear Road to drop off wagons for Helston. This was quicker as all the wagons to be detached were broad-gauge, although James noticed a set of mixed-gauge wagons being readied for the next up line train. St Erth was the final stop before Penzance and James was dropped off at his destination just after six in the evening. He set off to search for somewhere to live. He had been given two addresses to enquire at and found the first one quickly.

The door was opened after he had knocked several times and a small, barefoot child in a filthy dress looked out.

"We doan wan' any!" she said and shut the door.

James knocked again and this time a slattern opened the door, clearly the child's mother. "Wotcher want?" she asked.

James' mood sank; this didn't look at all the sort of place he wanted. From what he could glimpse inside the door, the place was quite foul. "Er – nothing, thank you," he said and hurried away. He might have to look for a hedge to sleep under for the night if the next place was similar.

But this time he had better luck; the lady at the door was elderly but pleasant, and the inside of the house seemed clean.

"Yis?" she asked.

"Er, I need accommodation," James said.

"Beg your pardon, my love?"

"Somewhere to live. I can pay," he added, holding out a shilling.

"Well, come in then."

He followed the lady into the house. It was small but tidy and well looked after. She showed him a room with a bed and a table and chair. There was a shelf for his things, a jug of water on the table, and a pot under the bed.

The conversation to discover her name and to arrange the rent took some time because her language was very difficult to follow, but finally he concluded that Mrs Tremethick was a widow whose husband had died in a tin mine some ten years earlier and that she had managed her life well enough without him by taking in the occasional lodger.

It was all very simple, but James didn't care; the stew she gave him for supper was tasty and after it he fell straight onto the bed and was asleep in seconds.

Next day, James woke up to a simple but nourishing breakfast of bread, cheese and well water. The bread was still warm from the oven; the elderly lady had baked it herself, he assumed, and it tasted better than any bread he had previously eaten.

On the Monday, he left after enjoying another welcome breakfast and Mrs Tremethick handed him a parcel of food wrapped in pastry.

"'Tes a pasty," she told him and went back into the house before he could ask what it contained.

He stuffed the pasty in his pocket and set off for the two-mile walk to Penzance Station. On his arrival, the shedmaster was welcoming.

"I'm glad to see you, young Baird. I was informed you were coming, and you'll be very useful. Now, have you somewhere to live?"

"Yes, sir."

"Good. You'll join a cleaning gang for a month then I'll decide on a more permanent position for you, depending on your progress."

"Sir."

James' cleaning gang was headed by Adam Newsome, a senior cleaner with a no-nonsense attitude. James soon discovered that although Cleaner Newsome was stern, he was fair.

In the first morning break, when James pulled out his pasty, another cleaner looked at it and remarked, "That looks like a fine pasty you've got there. What's in it?"

"I don't know," admitted James. "I've never seen anything like it before."

"You've never had a pasty?" Henry was surprised. "It's a Cornish meal, originally designed for tin miners."

"Tin miners?"

"Ar, the miner gets it from his missus, and he can have leftovers from yesterday's meal all wrapped up in pastry, so he can eat the wrapping as well. And–" Henry laughed – "if he drops it down the mine shaft, the pastry keeps everything together, like!"

James laughed as well, hoping that his own pasty wouldn't break his teeth. Later, he discovered that it tasted delicious; even the pastry had a pleasant flavour. Clearly, he was very fortunate to have Mrs Tremethick as a landlady.

"I'm Henry Newsome." James' fellow cleaner held out his hand and James shook it. "Grab your stuff and get busy on this engine's boiler."

James did as he was told and started to clean the boiler, glancing at the rest of the engine as he did so; it looked peculiar. It was a 2-4-0 with remarkably small wheels, side bunkers for the water but no tender for the coal. If it was a tender engine, where was the tender?

"Where is the coal?" he asked Henry curiously.

"On the bunkers on both sides," said Henry. "We'll fill it when it's cleaned and ready for service again."

As he worked, James wondered how far the engine would get before it needed more coal.

Henry watched him for a moment or two and then remarked; "You've cleaned engines before, haven't you? Where were you based?"

"Exeter," replied James. "I've been a cleaner there for over a year."

"Ah, the Bristol and Exeter Railway."

"Well, no, not really. The B & E was absorbed into the Great Western last year. So, I am a GWR employee."

"I see, well you'll soon get used to our ways," smiled Henry.

Yes, thought James, *or I hope I will. They have odd engines in West Cornwall, and they run trains with stock of different gauges in the same train. This next year or so is going to be interesting!*

7 - "How are the Mighty Fallen!" (Feb 1881)

It was a dreary day in early 1881 when the ex-Bristol and Exeter Railway 4-4-0 tank engine pulled into Watchet with a train from Minehead. Driver Herbert Parsons lowered the regulator, set the engine brake on, and spoke to his fireman, Alan Binks. "I'll be glad when they finally get rid of this broad gauge, Alan. Now that the Great Western has bought us out, we'll be changing to the narrow gauge right through the system."

"Why, Mr Parsons, what's wrong with our broad gauge?"

"It's out of its time, Alan, that's what. If they'd seen sense in 1846, we'd have kept it, but they didn't."

"I'm sorry, sir; I don't understand. I thought you didn't like the broad."

"Oh, there's nothing wrong in principle with the broad gauge, young feller; It's the confusion I don't like. From an engineering and economical point of view, our gauge is clearly superior; and the commissioners ought to have seen that, but by the time they drew their conclusions most of the kingdom's railways had already chosen Stephenson's gauge."

"Hmm. When I was a child, I was told that the broad gauge was smoother."

"Correct: it was. That was because Mr Brunel designed and built it well. But now that we are changing gauge, we haven't looked after the trackwork carefully and it's getting rough. We don't see that here of course, as our track is more recently laid, but on older lines it's getting no better than the narrow gauge. We don't repair it much; why spend money on maintenance when we know we are going to abandon it soon?"

"Yes, I see that."

"Now, have our passengers all boarded?"

Alan looked to see whether the guard had indicated the train was ready for departure but there seemed to be some kind of difficulty.

"Not yet, sir."

"Not yet? Why not?" Driver Parsons strolled over to see for himself what was causing the delay. Outside one of the carriages there was what seemed to be an angry discussion among a group of passengers. Parsons hurried over to the group and addressed the guard. "What's the problem here, Mr Saunders? This train has a timetable to keep!"

Guard Saunders pointed to a large passenger sitting in the carriage. "This passenger will not remove his ape, and the passengers won't board with his ape in the carriage."

"Ape?" Parsons couldn't believe his ears. "His ape?"

"He is a seaman just returned from Africa and he has brought an ape with him. He arrived in Cardiff and came over with the paddle steamer. He lives in Norton Fitzwarren, he says."

"And he has an ape with him?"

"He has; and the ape has a valid ticket." Parsons opened the carriage door and glanced inside. The portly seaman had a fully grown chimpanzee on the next seat; the animal was sitting quietly, holding its owner's hand. Herbert Parsons shook his head. He smiled at the seaman, shut the door and smirked at the guard. "You're in charge of the train, Mr Saunders, so it is for you to decide how to deal with it." And he walked back, grinning, to the cab.

"We have an unusual passenger today, Binks. An ape."

"A what?"

"An ape; about the size of a young boy. But don't worry; it has a ticket."

Alan could not decide whether his driver was joking but before he could think of a response, the guard's whistle sounded. Driver Parsons eased the locomotive brake, seized the regulator, and eased the train into motion.

"You did say an ape, Mr Parsons?"

"I did; it was with a seaman who had bought a ticket for it, but other passengers were unhappy with its presence in the carriage. I left the guard to settle the matter, which he seems to have done."

However, twenty minutes later, at Stogumber, there was a further delay, and shouting on the platform. Alan looked back and Parsons told him to go and find out how long they would be delayed this time. As Alan climbed down from the cab, he saw a seaman on the platform his with eyes firmly on the roof of a carriage, calling, "Come down, ye varmint!"

The chimpanzee was clutching the cylindrical shape of a gas vent. A number of passengers were following the proceedings with great interest, until the chimpanzee hurled an apple into the group and scuttled down the other side of the carriage, vanishing into some bushes with his owner climbing through a carriage to try and cut him off. Once the owner had also followed his animal into the bushes, the guard hurriedly sounded his whistle and Alan went quickly back to the cab.

"The matter seems to have been settled, Mr Parsons," he gasped breathlessly as he climbed up to the cab once more. "The animal has escaped," he explained.

"Excellent," remarked Driver Parsons. "Now we can start running a train properly." The rain which had been threatening for some time began to come down in earnest.

"Thankfully, we have a roof over our heads," commented his fireman, "and when we have narrow-gauge engines next year, I expect they too will have a cab with a roof."

"Don't get your hopes up on that, lad," warned Parsons. "Many new engines are still built with open cabs."

When they reached the main line west at Norton Fitzwarren, they noticed the heaps of building materials and tools being prepared for the gauge conversion of the line to Minehead.

"Not long now," remarked Parsons, "There's already plenty of mixed gauge in Devon and Cornwall and there's not been any broad-gauge trains north of Oxford for some years."

***

Driver Frederick Simmons had not been the happiest of men for some time. He enjoyed his job, no question; he was a top link driver based in Westbourne Park, the Great Western Railway's shed near Paddington, and now he spent most of his duties on the trains between Plymouth and Paddington using the old broad gauge main route to the west, on which he had spent most of his driving life. He had begun his career in Bristol, moving on to Plymouth until he had gained experience and transferred again to Reading, where he had to work north to Oxford and Wolverhampton, on narrow gauge engines in Wolverhampton. He had determined to transfer back to the broad gauge, driving on the roomy cabs of the bigger locomotives, and he duly did, to the main line west from Paddington.

The Great Western had for years fought the demand to convert in the face of increasing standard gauge mileage throughout the country. At first they proposed to add a third rail to their tracks in order to facilitate through traffic, but they had finally been forced to give way and had been converting the system gradually to standard gauge. The hitherto lauded superiority of the broad-gauge track was becoming an illusion.

Once the decision had been made to convert, little expense had been paid in maintaining the broad gauge's original superiority and by the early 1890s only the main line of 250 miles to Penzance was still broad, but everyone knew the end was near.

Frederick booked on to take a fast train to Bristol; there he would come off and return on a Paddington express. His engine was a Hawthorn class 2-4-0 engine and some of these were already twenty years old; some were still running in the late 1880s. Fortunately, Frederick's train was a light one and gave the locomotive no trouble on its way to Bristol. At Temple Meads Station, Fireman Mike Packard dropped to the track to uncouple, and Henry moved away for the ex-Bristol and Exeter Railway engine, another 2-4-0, to take over.

"One of these days, Mike," remarked Frederick to his fireman, gazing at both engines, "we'll have an engine with a roof on the cab and will be able to see where we're going even in heavy rain."

"Can't wait, Mr Simmons." Mike replied dryly; he did not sound optimistic.

The two men steamed slowly to the shed for their break and for their locomotive to be serviced. In two hours, they would be taking it back to Paddington. However, the servicing was slow and the shed foreman instructed them to take a different engine for the duty. This was another 2-4-0 which had been a narrow-gauge tank engine rebuilt to a broad-gauge engine and given a tender.

"We're in luck, Mr Simmons!" chortled Mike when he saw it. "It has a cab roof!" It was one of a number of narrow-gauge engines rebuilt for the broad gauge because of a shortage of broad-gauge engines.

"Mmmm," muttered Frederick. "I hope it's got the speed we want."

"Why shouldn't it have the power?" Mike was puzzled.

"It was a goods engine; they were not built for speed."

"We'll just have to see what we can do with it, then. I might have to bend my back a bit more today!"

Frederick's concern seemed prophetic; the engine drew away from Bristol easily but with the first steady uphill gradient her efforts effectively proved her hauling capability yet without any inclination to speed. Even on the few downhill sections before Swindon, she did not give the two men much hope for a timely arrival in Paddington.

Mike had by now been firing to Frederick for enough years for the driver to be prepared to allow him to drive from time to time and after leaving Swindon he decided Mike could benefit from a break from firing.

"Take the regulator for a spell, Mike, and I'll fire and give you a rest," said Frederick.

"Thank you Mr Simmons, I could use one," Mike said. He had been firing hard, to little effect on the speed. Frederick took the shovel and fired vigorously but quickly discovered that this engine was still not able to produce the speed they required for accurate timing.

"My Anna is going to have words when I get home tonight," grumbled Frederick. "And I promised Bill to read a story before his bedtime. They will both be upset."

Both men were quiet on the footplate as they tried to hurry their train, without avail. They pulled up at Paddington over an hour late. Henry explained to the shedmaster at Westbourne Park why.

"Yes, I am aware of the problem," replied the shedmaster.

"We are often short of good engines since Swindon stopped building broad gauge. But they are building some new engines for the narrow gauge which will be temporarily supplied with wheels outside their frames to run on the broad; the so-called 'convertibles'. These are beginning to emerge from Swindon, and I hope we will get one or two of them."

"Can't be soon enough for me and Fireman Packard," responded Frederick as he left for home.

They didn't have too long to wait.

One cool November morning in 1891, Frederick came into the enginemen's mess to discover that management had announced the final broad-gauge closure was to be made in May, and Frederick had only three more months to serve. He was not the only man to regret the end; many other drivers and firemen shared his affection for the wider gauge.

His duty that day was to take a morning express to Bristol. The engine was one of the brand-new Dean 2-2-2s; these engines were designed for the standard gauge but a few had been built to assist in the last months of the broad gauge, after which they would be converted to standard gauge locomotives. They were said by other drivers to be fast and powerful engines. Frederick climbed into the cab and saw Mike already busy there.

"Mornin' Mike. Any problems with the new engine?"

"Mornin' Mr Simmons; not as I can see; another forty minutes should see us fully ready."

"Right, I'll see to the oiling straightaway." Frederick took his oilcan with him and began to oil the motion.

The two men were busy for the next half-hour and Mike wondered whether they had time for a swift tea break. "What d'you think, Mr Simmons? Have we time for a quick mug?"

Frederick took out his watch. "Yes, if we're smart about it."

Once they had polished off their drinks, they took their engine out to the station to wait for the express coaches for Bristol. They arrived on time and the little tank engine which had hauled them from the carriage sidings uncoupled so that Frederick could back his own engine onto the train. In fifteen minutes, they were given the 'all clear' by the guard and Frederick eased the engine away, carefully trying to get the feel of this unfamiliar locomotive. There was very obviously no need to worry about power, he could sense that immediately.

Leaving the station, they rattled over the points with no effort, providing both men with a sense of relief.

"I believe we have a fine engine here, Mike," smiled Frederick as he accelerated the train towards Reading, some miles distant. Their locomotive responded instantly to Frederick's driving, and it wasn't long before they reached a speed which he believed would get them to Bristol on time, even allowing for the occasional signal check. Passing over Reading points, he was very surprised to see Mike spill a little coal on the cab floor. The fireman was usually meticulous in his maintenance of a clean cab; in fact, Frederick could not recall the last time Mike had done this and he stared at him in surprise. Admittedly they had felt a spot of poor track through Reading at one point but surely that wouldn't have put Mike off his swing?

"You feeling well, Mike?" he asked. "I haven't seen you spill coal for many years."

"Just caught me as I released the coal, Mr Simmons. That's a rough set of points we just went over."

Frederick raised his eyebrows. "But we often have that problem."

"Combination probably of the rough pointwork and my swing," Mike explained.

Frederick shook his head. This seemed possible, but he thought it was unlikely. He decided to keep a sharp eye on his mate. He hoped that Mike was not sickening for something.

But passing Bruton at high speed, Frederick had felt another slight jerk over some pointwork and wondered whether the platelayers had checked the track there; clearly something was amiss. He wondered whether Mike's problem with the spilled coal at Reading was also due to poor track. If so, he hadn't noticed it himself. He resolved to pay special attention to the track on the rest of their run to Bristol. It was quite possible, he mused, that track maintenance had been casual due to the imminent closure of the broad gauge. But even so, there was no excuse for dangerous track! What would the directors think if there were to be an accident? More importantly, what would the press have to say?

However, apart from a quiver inside Box tunnel, Frederick did not experience much in the way of uneven track. Even so, cleaning the cab after arriving in Temple Meads, Mike remarked that the rest of the run had been fine, but the distinct shudder in Box tunnel had worried him.

"Yes," replied Frederick, "I noticed that too. I'll put that in my report on the run before I forget it. The platelayers need to have a look at that section of track."

***

It was early May 1892 when Frederick, to his great regret, was informed that his final day before retirement would be a run on the broad gauge to Bristol and back. 21st May was the day before the last broad-gauge train was scheduled to leave Paddington. The regret was less that he was retiring and more that he was ending his long association with the broad gauge. In fact, the only pleasure he had was that he was to be driving one of the new Dean Singles again in his last duty. He and Mike prepared their engine, backed it into Paddington to the front of their train, and Mike descended and coupled it up before climbing back into the cab.

"We've got the guard's green, Mr Simmons," called Mike, leaning and looking back down the platform. As he spoke, the starter signal dropped and Frederick took the train easily out of the platform, accelerating gradually through the maze of pointwork of the Paddington approach. By the time they were passing Acton, the train was travelling at well over fifty miles per hour and running smoothly.

The rest of the duty to Bristol and return was such a thrill that Frederick was almost sorry he was retiring. *This new engine is a splendid machine*, he thought. But as they drew slowly back into Paddington Station, they noticed that most of the track was already converted to narrow gauge.

Both men were in the large crowd the following morning to watch the very last broad-gauge train leave for the west.

"'How are the mighty fallen!'" quoted Frederick as the train slowly left the station. "I'll never drive a broad-gauge engine again!"

"Wrong, I hope, Frederick." The quiet voice next to him belonged to Westbourne Park's shedmaster. "I've been looking for you. I have a request for you to stay on for another fortnight. We need a couple of experienced broad-gauge men to do some shunting at Swindon to marshal the existing rolling stock. Most will be scrapped but plenty will be converted. I've already got Henry Denton, and you have plenty of experience as well. Interested?"

Shunting was relatively easy work, and drivers could expect to be home on time every day, mused Frederick.

"Yes, sir. I'd be interested in an extra fortnight's pay, especially if it keeps the broad gauge alive for a little longer!"

8 - The New Broom
(Oct 1901)

Young Billy Carsons was firing the big Dean Single locomotive as it backed its way into the main down platform at Paddington. Driver Jonathon Surtees was grumbling, as was his wont, at the weather, the duty, the engine, or anything else that caught his eye that morning. In the five years as his mate, Billy had not once seen him smile, except for that one occasion when Driver Taylor had run into the stopblocks at Ranelagh Road, where visiting engines were serviced before returning to their own sheds. It was widely recognised at Old Oak Common engine shed that the two drivers loathed each other, but nobody could explain why, and neither man was prepared to elaborate on the details. The many suggestions were both plausible as well as impossible (although the latter were usually highly diverting).

It was nevertheless acknowledged that Driver Surtees was a competent driver in any cab the Great Western could offer him, and he was forgiven his irascibility because he was paternally inclined to his young firemen, although this attitude did not apply to those in his cab who used coarse language or abused their betters.

On this late autumn day, it was raining hard and had been for some time as Driver Surtees eased the Plymouth express out of the trainshed at Paddington Station. The train was only moderately heavy - eight coaches only as it was past the mild autumn days and heading into winter - and consequently gave the locomotive little trouble in starting. This was one of the fast Dean express engines with the single huge driving wheels on each side; these engines were often referred to as 'runners' by older drivers because once they had got hold of a train they could run at high speed.

"We may have trouble today, Billy," muttered Surtees as they eased out of the station. "Trains are getting heavier and these runners are not coping as well as they used to. I took some of the first ones on the old broad gauge and they were excellent then, even without the front bogie."

"Why did they add that bogie then, Mr Surtees?" asked Billy curiously as he checked the firebox.

"They were unstable at speed, and one came off the road in a tunnel, so they decided to replace the front pony truck with a bogie," explained his driver.

"But they seem to be managing well enough now," remarked Billy as they left the overall roof of the vast trainshed. But just as Billy spoke, there came an almighty roar as the huge driving wheels reached the wet rails and spun round, shaking the whole engine before Surtees could react. Immediately he lowered the regulator to slow the speed and reduce the noise; he operated the sanders and tried again. Once more, the engine slipped and spun the wheels without making much progress; Surtees tried again and this time the driving wheels retained some grip on the sanded rails and the train slowly began to move, and by the time they had left the platform, they had the train under control again. The inertia and weight of the train made the locomotive's job slightly easier, and Driver Surtees was able to accelerate the express to an acceptable rate.

"Now see what your distraction did to me," grumbled Surtees.

"Sorry, Mr Surtees," said a chastened Billy, "I wasn't thinking."

"Not good enough, young man. In the cab you always have to keep your wits about you," replied Surtees, ignoring the fact that he himself had not been concentrating on his driving. Even so, the engine was still not pulling as Surtees had come to expect and he was wondering why; it was less than ten years old and one of the newer ones, not ones that had been built originally for the broad gauge. The class had been constructed in the expectation that the broad gauge would soon be closed so only the first few had been constructed as broad-gauge engines with a planned alteration to standard gauge later. Were the coaches packed with passengers or were they newer and heavier coaches? If so, why had the guard not informed him?

They hurried past Old Oak Common shed and since their speed had now reached its normal level, Surtees' mind reverted to its normal, somewhat pessimistic, view of life in general. The dismal late October weather was not conducive to cheerful thinking, not that such was Surtees' inclination anyway, and he began to wonder whether he was getting too old for driving. This was a worry because he usually enjoyed the job and knew that he was still good at it. He was also aware that Her Majesty was also becoming difficult and reclusive if the papers were to be believed; even *The Times*, normally very reserved regarding matters concerning the Crown, had mentioned Government difficulties in communicating with the Queen at Osborne House on the Isle of Wight.

"Some of the firemen are saying that Mr Dean will be retiring soon," remarked Billy as he replaced his shovel to check the steam pressure gauge, "and that Mr Churchward will replace him."

"I've heard that too," said Surtees. Mr Dean was said not to be well and leaving important decisions to Churchward, his deputy; it was also rumoured that he was slowly losing his grasp of affairs, but Surtees did not mention that to his fireman.

The young man's grins on gossip about Prince Edward's attentions to high society ladies verged, Surtees feared, on disrespect for the great and the good, and that did not at all meet with his approval. And what was worse was that the lad did not see any harm in this attitude; such a viewpoint could only lead to communism or anarchy! Surtees shook his head at the innocence of the young. Was it not his duty to attempt to correct such foolishness?

In spite of these thoughts, Surtees automatically kept his eye on the job; he didn't want any repetition of a distraction and another lack of concentration leading to a further mistake. He didn't like to think of what his colleagues back in Old Oak Common shed were already going to say when he returned. They would by then all have heard of that embarrassment on leaving Paddington, and the wits there would have a good deal to say about it! Yet by the time they were passing Slough, Surtees wondered whether he had been unduly pessimistic about these Achilles class 4-2-2 engines: his was now running well and keeping time. He was sure that, barring incidents, they would arrive in Reading right time, and he could then note down the details in his driver's notebook. He glanced over to see how Billy was coping, but there was no need to worry there either. The lad had developed a neat swing with the firebox doors and the shovel with coal straight into where it was needed; he still had quite a lot to learn but was obviously going to make a very competent driver in the not-too-distant future.

The weather on their approach to their first stop at Reading was not promising; there were heavy clouds, and it was still raining. Surtees would need to take care on leaving; he really didn't want a repeat wheel-spin as the engine tried to get hold of the heavy train on the wet rails. It would be simply far too embarrassing to request a pilot engine to take the train out!

He turned quickly to Billy while the passengers were still boarding. "Quick, Billy, slip down to the track ahead with your shovel and throw some of the sand falling out of the sanders when I work them and move out slowly along the rails. Don't worry, I'll be slow enough for you to jump up again, once the engine has her train in hand."

Billy nodded and as soon as the guard's whistle sounded, he dropped down to the track and began to shovel some of the sand falling down by the side of the rails onto the rail surface ahead as the train moved slowly forwards. This went on for about twenty yards until he heard a call from the cab. "Righto, Billy!" whereupon he threw his shovel onto the cab floor and scrambled back up, grinning. "I've never done that before, Mr Surtees!"

"It won't be the last time either, youngster," replied Surtees. "Many's the time as a fireman, I had to run beside a train, shovelling any bits of rubbish from the track onto the rails to allow the driving wheels to get a grip on the rails! You'll be doing it again soon enough!"

Billy frowned, "But wouldn't big stones from the ballast break up and fire shards across your legs?"

Surtees nodded, "Yes, stones from ballast aren't the best thing; you need to look for smaller stones for preference. They crush more easily and give greater support. You can usually find them at the side of the track."

Fortunately, the weather had cleared up by the time they reached Didcot, their next stop, and there was no drama on leaving again; however, their engine once again began to show signs of labouring, and Surtees was beginning to wonder whether he would need a pilot at Swindon. But whether it was Billy's hard work at the firebox or Surtees' skill on the regulator, they reached Swindon without indicating any apparent need for assistance. *Only two more sticky stretches,* thought Surtees, *the bank after Taunton then the South Devon banks after Exeter. If Billy was more experienced, I'd give him a spell on the regulator but he's still far too young yet. Pity.*

But it seemed that Lady Luck was on their side that day: the rear coach developed a hot axlebox and had to be taken off at Taunton, which eased the load on the train by over thirty tons. The passengers were annoyed of course, but it couldn't be helped; there was no spare coach available until Plymouth, they were informed. The pause at Taunton to uncouple the coach provided Billy with time to give the fire the attention needed for the coming bank, and Surtees was able to take the express away with no trouble. With a lighter load, they ascended the bank without any ordeal on Billy's part, and the later South Devon banks were similarly dealt with. Nevertheless, Surtees was glad when they arrived in Plymouth.

"I'm beginning to think that some of the other drivers might be right about these Dean engines," he said to Billy. "They are perhaps not tackling the heavy trains as well as they did."

"But what better engines for the heavy expresses have we got?" asked Billy. "I can't think of any."

"No, you're quite right there. We do need more powerful engines."

The death of Queen Victoria four months later took their minds temporarily off the worry about increasing train weights, and the nation mourned the loss of their old queen and empress; she had reigned for sixty-three years.

"Now we have to get used to our new monarch, Edward VII, whose attitude to life is totally different," grumbled Surtees to Billy one morning as he heard the news. "Things at court are about to change radically!"

He and his fireman were waiting at Laira locomotive shed in

Plymouth to take their engine to Plymouth's Millbay Station and return on a Paddington express.

Surtees' remark could, it seemed, be equally applied at the Great Western Railway. George Jackson Churchward was appointed new chief mechanical engineer, and very different engines began to appear. A range of 4-4-0s with varying wheel sizes were proving to be very capable and fast engines, and one of them was their own engine for the up Paddington express. It was a City class 4-4-0 and as they backed it down onto the coaches of their train, Surtees began to smile; he could sense the power it appeared to have.

"I've never driven one of these, Billy, but I'm looking forward to the run today."

Billy looked at him in astonishment. The driver was actually smiling! He didn't know how to reply, so he simply nodded and checked the fire once again. He didn't have much to smile about: the run to Newton Abbot was over the fearsome hills of South Devon and was no fun for any fireman. But the new locomotive, once it put its nose up into the first rising gradient, proved to be more than capable of the hills with a half competent fireman, and Billy felt personally rewarded as the engine managed the train without undue effort, and rolled into Newton Abbot on time.

Surtees, Billy noticed, was smiling again, perhaps at the thought of what the new engine could do down the bank into Taunton. This was a well-tried racing section, and many a driver couldn't resist the temptation to run down at high speed. Driver Surtees was no exception, and since Billy didn't need to fire for a few minutes, he tried to count the passing telegraph poles to guess at their speed. He didn't succeed but he knew for sure that they were faster than they had ever been before.

"We're going to slow a little, Billy," remarked Surtees, smiling after they had passed Taunton. "We don't want to get into Bristol ahead of time; an inspector will want to know why!"

But at Bristol Surtees' smile vanished. On the down main platform opposite they saw a Plymouth express standing with Driver Taylor grinning at them from the cab of a new 4-6-0.

"You're late again, Surtees!" he called over. "Can't you handle an express engine?" He chortled.

Surtees drew his notebook from the cab roof and waved it at Taylor. "One minute and forty seconds ahead of time, Taylor," he replied and pointed at the platform clock. "But look at the clock; you're four minutes late. It's you who can't handle an express engine!"

"Guard's whistle, Mr Surtees," spoke Billy quietly, looking backwards out of the cab. Surtees nodded and, ignoring Taylor, eased the brake off and lifted the regulator gently and the locomotive began to move off slowly but firmly.

"I have no time for that man," he declared.

Ninety minutes later immediately before passing Swindon Works a distant signal was at caution and Surtees slowed in preparation to stop at the next home signal. As they trundled past the works, Billy gasped. "Look at that engine; It's a monster!" It had a long, coned boiler, inside frames, six driving wheels and outside cylinders. There was a second next to it but this, although it was the same size, had a 4-4-2 wheel arrangement.

Surtees glanced briefly over. "I imagine that's Mr Churchward at work; he's trying his own designs. We'll be in one of those engines within a few years, I shouldn't wonder."

Surtees was quite right. Only five years later, he and Billy found themselves in the cab of one of the new 4-6-0 express passenger engines. The difference was remarkable; they had been pleased with the City engines but now even these were beginning to reach their limit as the weight of traffic increased again.

One morning at Paddington, they were rostered to take a Bristol express and a new 4-6-0 from Old Oak Common shed backed on to the train where Surtees and Billy were waiting.

The servicing enginemen climbed down from the cab. "She's all yours, Jonathon, and you'll love her!" beamed the driver. "I wish I was taking her to Bristol!" Then he and his fireman left them to return to the shed.

Climbing into the cab, Driver Surtees and Billy found the controls very similar to what they were used to; Churchward had standardised cab layouts as far as possible so that changing locomotives did not cause needless problems.

The guard came up to the cab. "You got ten on, Mr Surtees, 300 tons."

Surtees nodded; this was a heavy train. He would see how the new engine would handle this weight. Fifteen minutes later, the green flag was waved and the starter signal dropped. Surtees took the engine gently at first to get used to the feel and then eased the speed up slightly and the locomotive responded instantly, with no hesitation. *This looks very promising*, he thought as he accelerated out of Paddington round the left curve. *I'm glad Billy is getting to be a competent and reliable fireman; it won't be long before I can trust him with a short spot of driving along an easy stretch.*

Within the first twenty minutes, Surtees was certain the guard had given him the wrong train weight; their engine was managing the load with ease. Approaching a left-hand curve, he asked Billy to count the coaches.

"I think the guard gave me the wrong number," he explained, "she's not straining at all under the weight."

Billy counted. "No, we've got ten coaches, Mr Surtees," he said.

"Are you sure?"

"Yes, I counted twice." Surtees shook his head at Billy's response. "We have a very fine engine, then. It's making the job look easy."

The stops at Reading and Didcot on time with no signs of strenuous effort from the engine convinced Surtees that with this new engine they had something special. The rest of the run to Bristol, Taunton, Exeter, Newton Abbot and then Plymouth was a trip such that Surtees in all his driving had never experienced. This new locomotive would pull a heavy train and run like the wind when required; it was a revelation.

Their return to London the next day was with another City class 4-4-0 and, although it was a satisfactory run, it did not have the magic of the previous day with the new 4-6-0. It was soon clear, however, that a fleet of new 4-6-0 locomotives was taking over the heavy expresses and taking the new two-hour expresses to Birmingham with no trouble.

"Twenty years back, Billy," said Surtees to his fireman as they pulled up in Snow Hill on time a year or so later, "I thought that our Dean Singles were unbeatable, but Mr Churchward is like a new broom sweeping away all the dross we had. You'll be a happy driver soon able to manage any of these great engines!"

But Surtees was not quite accurate in this prophecy. There were political clouds on the horizon which were to cause a great war and impose enormous strains on all the nation's railway companies, and even Mr Churchward's magnificent engines could not solve the Great Western's problems.

9 - The Mighty Monarchs
(June 1927)

As the regulator in his locomotive jammed for third time that morning, Ifan Pew - tank engine driver of the Taff Vale Railway - swore out loud. He reached round to the toolbox behind him, grabbed a hefty spanner, and tapped the handle of the regulator down. The engine began to slow its progress down the steep valley.

"You wouldn't believe that the war ended nine years ago, Emrys," Driver Pew growled, lowering the regulator gingerly. "We still haven't had the bloody repairs properly done. I don't think they'll get round to 'em until we have an accident!"

Fireman Emrys Jones nodded his agreement, adding, "I don't think much of these new GWR tank engines Collett has foisted on us either." Both men spoke in Welsh, like many of their colleagues in the South Wales valleys. "They might be brand new, but they've got their problems. Last week, when I was with Johnny Robson, we had one of them derail on the entrance to the shed at the docks! Closed every movement in and out 'til we got her back on the road again. Boss was livid!"

"I bet he was! He's got a short fuse, has the boss!" Ifan Pew smiled.

The train slowed down further as they began to round the left-hand curve after passing Tongwynlais, ready for the stop at the next station at Radyr, where several ladies with their shopping bags were ready to board for their day's shopping in nearby Cardiff. Ifan had one hand on the regulator as he looked behind him through the rear spectacle plate towards the approaching platform. Drivers with these 0-6-2T engines generally drove their trains with the bunker facing downhill because the rear pony wheels gave better guidance round the many curves.

"I hope that derailed engine wasn't this one," muttered Ifan.

"Very unlikely," chuckled Emrys as he threw another shovelful of coal into the firebox. "This doesn't look like—" He paused as he noticed an unusual green fleck on the paint under the window. *Where have I seen that before?*

"Diew, Ifan! it was this engine!" he called.

But just as he spoke, the locomotive lurched to the right as the leading pony truck came off the track, followed by the leading pair of driving wheels. As it had already slowed down considerably, the rest of the engine stayed on the rails, albeit coming to a rapid stop with a jerk, followed by another, as the inertia of the four coaches added their weight, shoving the train a few yards on. Fortunately nothing else derailed, but there were shouts and yells from behind as the passengers were shaken about.

Ifan instantly shut off steam, glancing quickly around to see whether his fireman was hurt. "You alright, Emrys?"

A swearing Emrys picked himself up from the cab floor. "This bloody engine doesn't like me, Ifan!" he snarled as he moved to the cab doorway. "I'll go and see whether any passengers or the guard are injured." He climbed down and hurried along to the rear coach.

The guard was already climbing out. "What the hell's happened, Emrys?"

"We've derailed, Ianto, but the engine is still on the rails and upright. Ifan's fine, but we need to check the passengers."

"Right! Let's get busy!"

It took half an hour to ascertain that nobody was seriously injured, although several passengers were taken to hospital for further observation while the railway repair gang arrived, jacking the engine up to rerail it. A spare engine from Cardiff was sent up haul to the locomotive with its train down to Cardiff Queen Street, from where the engine was taken back to the works.

***

Driver Norman Smeddle from Old Oak Common shed glanced down at the platform at Paddington then looked at his fireman as they slowly backed their Castle onto its train.

"You had plenty of nourishing porridge this morning, Jeff?" he asked with a grin. "We seem to have a heavy load today!"

"Shouldn't be a problem with our Castle, surely, Norm," Fireman Anson smiled. "Two and a half hours to 'hampton isn't too much to ask."

Driver Smeddle's eyebrows lifted in surprise. "Near five hundred tons on a hilly road?"

Jeff Anson lifted his arms and flexed his muscles. "A new Castle and these two?" he grinned. "Piece of cake!"

"I'll wait to watch you show your muscles to the Chester crew when they relieve us in 'hampton," Smeddle responded, amused, "then I'll be convinced! Now hop down and couple us up to the train."

Anson climbed down and stood on the platform to indicate how close the engine was to the coaches, began to raise his hand slowly as his driver closed the gap, then dropped it suddenly. Smeddle stopped the locomotive's movement and started again, easing it until there was a gentle bump as the tender buffers met those of the foremost coach. Anson lifted the huge coupling loop, dropped it over the hook, tightened it, then connected the vacuum brake and steam heating pipes before climbing back into the cab to check the firebox.

In the meantime, the guard came up to the cab, calling up, "Norman, you've got sixteen on, and each one is as full as a sardine tin! You've got nearly 560 tons!"

Hearing this, Anson winced quietly but took care not to show his concern to his driver.

"Sixteen? God in his Heaven! We'll be lucky to make it to Banbury, Arthur!"

"Think of me having to look after them all; anyway, you'll slip a coach at Bicester."

"Of course; I'd forgotten that. Thanks, Arthur!" Smeddle took out his notebook and noted down the details; they were due out in fifteen minutes.

As the platform clock clicked over to ten minutes past nine, the guard sounded his whistle and Anson, looking back along the platform, called, "We've got the green, Norm!"

Smeddle lifted the regulator and eased the brakes, and the heavy train began to make its way out, weaving across the points and crossings of the Paddington approaches set for the down main line out of London. Minutes later, passing Westbourne Park, Smeddle pointed to the tender and remarked, "Ten years back, Jeff, I bet you never thought you'd ever be shovelling railway coal again!"

Anson looked up from his shovelling. "No Norm, you're quite right; whenever that damned whistle went and I grabbed my rifle to jump out of the trench, I used to wonder where the bullet would hit me. I never dreamed I'd get back to Blighty!"

"And here you are with a driver's exam not too far ahead of you!"

"Good grief. Don't remind me!" Jeffrey Anson had been firing for fifteen years now, aside from a three-year interruption as a soldier during the Great War, and had recently been told by his shed foreman to be prepared to sit his driver's exam. He had been studying the rule book avidly.

"I'm sure we'll manage after yesterday's run, Norm." He turned his attention back to the task in hand. He knew his driver was right: Paddington trains to Wolverhampton were getting heavy. Mr Churchward, their widely respected chief mechanical engineer, had retired four years earlier having given the Great Western a fleet of engines. The Stars and Saints were the envy of many other companies, but with the trains getting heavier, the new chief mechanical engineer, Charles Collett, had developed and enlarged a Star class engine and produced an even stronger locomotive, the Castle class, which the enginemen had taken to with delight. It could run like a Star and was even more powerful.

"Aye, we will," replied Smeddle, "but we are not the only company with problems. I was talking to a Swindon draughtsman last week when I was on a Bristol express, and he said the LMS had asked us to build them fifty Castles! We told 'em we couldn't build enough ourselves! We wouldn't even give them our drawings!"

"That right?"

"Yep, and what's more, he said Mr Collett is looking at a bigger Castle himself!"

"Blimey!" breathed Jeffrey. "And we've only just rebuilt our

Great Bear Pacific into a Castle! Why didn't they make that more powerful?"

"It kept falling off the track."

"It was an ugly-looking bugger anyway." Jeffrey had clearly been unimpressed with the big engine. "That huge, long boiler and the tiny cab stuck on at the back looked ridiculous, I thought. Did you ever drive it?"

"Yeah, a couple of times; it couldn't do more than a Star anyway, I found. It was very restricted in where they could run it, so when the boiler needed attention they decided to rebuild it as a Castle anyway."

"Mmm," Fireman Anson pondered, "but I fired to Freddy Worksop last month on a down Wolverhampton with fifteen on, and they were heavily loaded; it was a bugger of a duty to get 'em to 'hampton. We were fortunate to be able to slip two at Bicester. Freddy's a good driver but even he was worried about losing time."

"Yes, I've had the same situation myself once recently and I didn't enjoy it either, but there's a rumour that Swindon is looking at the problem seriously."

What neither man knew was that Charles Collett had finalised the drawings of his new, powerful engine, and Swindon was already building it. After Halls, Abbeys, and now Castles, GWR management had decided on Cathedrals for the names of their new powerful locomotives.

"When he does," responded Anson, "it'll probably be a Pacific like the one we just lost; the LNER likes 'em."

"We'll just have to wait and see."

They didn't have to wait long, and the new engines were not Pacifics but larger 4-6-0s like the Castles, and they were not Cathedrals but Kings. (Someone had leaked the Cathedral name to the press.) The GWR had asked the Palace whether they could use the names of kings, and the request had been granted.

King George V took to the rails in June 1927 for trials before being shipped over to the United States to the Baltimore and Ohio Railway Exhibition as a static exhibit. Later, it steamed there, and greatly impressed the Americans.

"Lookit that li'l engine!" commented one spectator. "Tidy lookin' and pulls jest as well as one of our monsters! How do the Brits do it?"

One or two American locomotives even appeared later with copper-capped chimneys.

***

Driver Joseph Oakleigh at Wolverhampton's Stafford Road shed was an unusual man. He was an experienced and competent driver – no surprise there, the Stafford Road had plenty of those – but he had a coarse manner coupled with a curiously rigid Christian conviction, which would have led to occasional teasing had it not been for Joe's readiness to use his fists. Oakleigh's firemen were well aware of the driver's beliefs and took great care not to offend him. Joe also had an avid interest in the oddities of history. The only driver able to tease him and get away with it was Jasper Smollett, who was good-natured and normally able to divert Joe's anger by his gentle teasing.

One lunchtime, Driver Oakleigh and his fireman, Tom Butcher, were preparing their Castle to take over a Birkenhead as far as Chester from the Old Oak Common Castle which they expected would bring it in from Paddington. Oakleigh was just finishing oiling the motion.

"All coaled and trimmed, Butcher?" he called.

"Yep," came the reply from the cab.

"It'd better be! Steam pressure ready?" Oakleigh glanced at his watch. They were due off the shed in five minutes.

"Yeah; close to blowing off!"

Oakleigh climbed back into the cab. "Right, I'll get 'er movin' then."

Just as he was about to release the brake, a call came from the ground.

"Joe, give us a lift to the station, will you?"

Oakleigh saw Driver Jasper Smollett and Fireman Harry Forsyth; they were to take an express to Paddington.

"Can't yer walk? Hop up then, yer lazy buggers."

Both men climbed up for the short run to the station.

As they backed in on the siding ready for their changeover, they saw their train arriving behind what looked like a Castle, but there was something different about the front of the engine. It looked odd: the boiler front was larger and there was something different about the front bogie.

"What the 'ell's that?" Oakleigh was puzzled.

"That, Joe, is one of our new monarchs," explained Jasper. "I saw one at Paddington two days back."

"Monarchs?"

"Kings, dear boy, Kings!"

"Kings eh? Very 'igh an' mighty!" scoffed Oakleigh, as the new King uncoupled and moved slowly past, showing its nameplate: *King James I*.

Jasper looked at it with interest. "Ah, the king with your Bible, Joe!"

"King James' Bible? Rubbish! The Bible's the word of God!" Oakleigh was offended.

"Oh?" Jasper's eyebrow rose in apparent surprise. "Is God English?"

"What?"

Jasper explained as if to a child. "We can read the Bible because it's in English."

Joe frowned, "Oh yeah, I s'pose some bugger translated it."

"Yes," replied Jasper, "it was Tyndale. James the First and Sixth didn't like Tyndale's translation and set up a committee to make a better one."

"Is that right? Any'ow, wot did yer— 'ang on; first and sixth? 'Ow c'd James be both?"

"Take it from me, Joe, he was."

"Yer talkin's shit. Wot about Jimmies two, three, four an' five?"

"Oh, they died before James the First was King of England."

"Now ye're talkin' total bollocks!"

"I'll tell you something else, too: he was James the Sixth before he was James the First!"

Joe glared at Jasper then pointed out of the cab. "Piss off, the pair of yer!"

Luckily, they had reached the platform and, chuckling, Jasper left the cab with Harry.

On the platform Harry, glancing at Jasper, said, "I don't like Joe Oakleigh any more than you do, Jasp, but he's got a point.

That did sound like bollocks."

Jasper grinned. "Yes, I couldn't help pulling his leg, Harry. It's a paradox but all perfectly true. Elizabeth died in 1603 and had no children that they knew of, so the next in line for the English crown was King James the Sixth of Scotland, but England hadn't had a King James, so he was known as James the First and Sixth." Jasper smiled. "He was, therefore, James the Sixth before he was James the First!"

By this time, they had reached the public cafeteria. "I'll treat you to tea and a sticky bun, Harry. We have plenty of time before we pick up our engine for the Paddington. My guess is that we'll be taking that King back."

"Really? I'd certainly enjoy firing a King; they're said to be good engines. It would be nice to find out for myself."

They ate in eager anticipation as their King, having been turned and serviced, arrived with its strengthening coaches on the up main, ready for them to take over the Paddington express.

Fifteen minutes later, their train from Birkenhead had arrived and the Castle bringing it in uncoupled and left for the shed. They backed their King and its coaches onto the train and Harry climbed down to couple up. Jasper gazed in interest round the cab as he waited for Harry to return. Apart from the new paint smell, it was hard to distinguish it from that of a Castle.

However, Jasper sensed the power of the new engine as they backed onto their train with the six extra coaches; it felt like the locomotive was gliding rather than steaming.

The train from Birkenhead was a heavy one; it had left Birkenhead with seven, three more had been attached in Chester, and now it had sixteen on. The shed staff had serviced the King well, and the fire was burning nicely. Harry wriggled his shoulders to loosen them; he was expecting to have to shovel hard for the next three hours or so.

The guard's whistle sounded, the starter signal dropped, and Jasper took hold of the regulator and eased it upwards, slowly and carefully. The response from the engine was incredible: the speed with which it moved off was almost the same as it had shown hauling only the six coaches.

"Crikey, Jasp; didn't the guard tell us we had sixteen on?"

"He did indeed, Harry. Impressive, isn't it?"

Twenty minutes later, having threaded their way through the Black Country, they arrived in Birmingham Snow Hill, their initial impression confirmed: they had a magnificent engine. Hurrying south through the suburbs of Bordesley, Tyseley, Acocks Green, Knowle and Dorridge, they had little chance to show any real speed, but as they were signalled clear through to Leamington Spa, their first stop, the locomotive showed no sign of the weight of its train.

"Another half-hour to Banbury, Harry, and then we'll be able to open her up a little," said Jasper. "Non-stop to Paddington over the Chilterns will give us an idea of what she's capable of."

He was looking forward to being able to see for himself what the new engine could do.

After they left the last stop at Banbury, they were soon into the Chilterns and climbing, but the sixteen coaches seemed to make little difference to their King; the locomotive was eating away the miles with ease and during one of his brief rests Harry was able to smile as he looked out of the cab.

This stretch of track was where the up and down main lines were separate from one another, and they appeared to be racing along a single track as if this were a branch line. Jasper noticed that according to the speedometer they touched 90mph at least once on the run down to the London approaches and their arrival in Paddington was one minute early.

At the Paddington stop blocks, Jasper leaned back and turned to Harry. "We now have an engine which will handle our heaviest trains for years!"

He was quite right.

In fact, the Kings handled the heaviest expresses and were even improved in the late 1950s. They were nearly all withdrawn (with years of life left in them) in 1962, almost at the end of steam on the Western because there was no more work for them as the diesels came in. The Kings had served the Western well for close to forty years.

10 - Driver Denton's New Mate
(April 1936)

Shed Foreman Sidney Thomson had asked Driver Denton to take on a young cleaner as a fireman for a spell and give his opinion on the lad.

"Other drivers have told me he's got promise," explained the shedmaster. "I want to know what you think. He's a passed cleaner, George, so he's permitted to fire with an experienced driver, other things being equal, so to speak."

"What's his name, Sid?"

"He's Passed Cleaner Lance Hargreaves."

"Oh yes, I've seen him about." George smiled. "I've heard him too: he's not afraid to give his cleaner mates an earful from time to time when he thinks they deserve it, so I know about his language. I've also heard he's a lecherous young devil too."

"Yes, that's right. I was told he even gave Fireman Smith some lip the other day."

"Marty Smith? I bet the lad regretted that! Marty's not one to take cheek from a young cleaner!"

"Oddly enough, Smith admitted his fault, then he gave young Hargreaves a very firm dressing-down. He told him another fireman might have given him a thick ear and that authority would back up the senior man regardless!"

George laughed. "I hope the lad's learned from that. Marty always seems to have a beef about something, but he's not a bad fireman and one day he could make a good driver. Anyway, Sid, I'll take on young Hargreaves and let you know what I think."

In the ensuing days, George's opinion of his new fireman firmed into an appreciation of the lad's potential. Lance had, it seemed to George, a real gift for work in an engineman's cab. He merely needed careful honing, and Driver Denton thought he knew how to encourage this. However, he was less sure about what could be done about the boy's language, which was earthy, often in the extreme.

He had little doubt too about his fireman's lechery and this was demonstrated one day on the early shift. They were booked on a short parcels train to Central Wales one morning, leaving at five-forty; they were to crew it as far as Ruabon, where an Oswestry crew would take over. Lance was firing through Rossett when he sneezed suddenly. He put his shovel down and took out a handkerchief to blow his nose and, as he tried to push his hanky back into his pocket, he sneezed again and the cloth fell to the cab floor near George's foot. George leaned down to pick it up gingerly by a corner and hand it back when it fell open to reveal itself not as a normal handkerchief, but a pair of frilly knickers.

George stared at the lad. "Late night last night, was it, Lance?"

"Um – yes, Mr D." Lance shook his head in embarrassment and stuffed the item back into his pocket. He was learning to respect his driver and didn't want to disappoint him. George merely shook his head sadly but said nothing, thinking guiltily about his own adventures when on leave in Paris during the Great War. But since he had married his Alice twelve years previously, he'd had no interest in any other woman.

On their return, George and Lance were returning from Wellington with an older Aberdare class 2-6-0 on a Birkenhead freight and were slowly trundling through Wrexham Station, hoping the next signal would show clear. Lance glanced over to see a large, and very clean, Prairie class 2-6-2T on an up local passenger train standing at the up main platform. He noticed with interest that Passed Cleaner John Fletcher, one of his older colleagues, was firing.

John saw him at the same time and yelled across, grinning. "Bin demoted ter firin' a tin can, 'ave yer, Lance, yer lazy sod?"

Annoyed, Lance yelled back, "Me tin can's made o' good steel, Fletch. An' 'oo's a lazy sod then? Me couplin's 'ooked up proper at the front, not like yours!"

Front couplings of Great Western locomotives were supposed to be hooked up so that they didn't swing loose during running, and this was the fireman's duty.

Unfortunately for young Fletcher, his driver was a stickler for the rules and heard the taunt. Driver Hardcastle grabbed his fireman by the ear. "Get down and fix that coupling, you idle young bugger!"

Rubbing his ear, Fletcher climbed down to lift the coupling onto the hook provided for it. He saw Lance watching and lifted two fingers to him. Lance returned the gesture with a broad grin.

The signal dropped to 'clear' and Driver Denton lifted the regulator. The Aberdare accelerated on its journey northwards again.

"You don't like that lad, do you, Lance?" George remarked.

"No, Mr D, ter be honest, I don't. 'E's always tryin' ter put people down. Never 'as a good word fer anyone, 'cept 'imself o' course."

George shook his head. He agreed with Lance but was surprised at John Fletcher. *Hasn't the young fool learned that teasing Lance always brings a negative response?* He respected Eric Hardcastle and knew that he dealt with his firemen fairly, as long as they were competent, and seriously doubted that young Fletcher would enjoy his time with the driver. If he ever became a driver himself, George thought, Fletcher's firemen were in for a rough time. They'd get little help from him and no assistance with the firing if the run was a tough one.

As they passed Gresford, George said, "You can take things a little easier here for a few minutes, Lance, the engine can run down the bank without much pushing. In fact, you may have to drop out and put a few of the wagon brakes on to stop the inertia from pushing the train too fast. I'll tell you if it's necessary."

"What's inersha then, Mr D?"

"It's the force of the weight that builds up in the train and it can even overcome the braking force of the weight of the locomotive and tender."

"Yer mean the wagons c'n push the train down'ill even with the engine brake on?" Lance found this difficult to understand.

"Think about it, Lance, how much does our engine with its tender weigh?"

"Er - round a 'undred tons?"

"Yes, that's close enough. What does our loaded freight train weigh?"

"Could be three 'undred? Cripes, yeah; it could weigh more'n twice wot the engine weighs."

"And that's why freights have a heavy guard's van; the guard can use its braking weight to help slow the train when needed."

Lance bent to shovel more coal into the firebox. "Dunno why ye're not a university perfesser, Mr D," he remarked with a grin.

George chuckled as they had reached the bottom of the bank and the train's inertia would assist acceleration as he eased the brake off. They began to pick up speed again over the flatter area just south of Chester.

This young lad might be rough around the edges, but he's quick and intelligent, thought George. *If he carries on like this, he could make a cracking driver one day. Pity about his language!*

As they ran slowly down the bank, Lance asked, "D'yer want me ter nip out and slip a few o' the wagons' brakes, Mr D?"

George stared at him. "What did I tell you, Lance?"

"Er – yer said yer'd let me know if I was ter nip out an' put a few wagon brakes on."

"Correct; and have I let you know?"

"Er – no."

"So why did you ask me?"

Lance paused. "Dunno, Mr Denton."

For the first time, George had caught Lance without a response. He decided to drop the subject: he had made his point and saw no need to rub the lad's nose in it.

There was silence in the cab for the next few miles, but approaching Saltney, George warned Lance to be ready for a hard pull up the gradient before they joined the North Wales main line, to continue their run to Chester. Curiously, the mile and a half between Saltney Junction and Chester was LMS property but the GWR had to pay for the running powers over it, whereas Chester General Station and the line to Birkenhead were jointly owned by both companies.

They took the Chester avoiding line round past the station and onto the Birkenhead line, with Lance studiously firing carefully and checking the water and steam pressure. George watched him unobtrusively and approved of the way the young passed cleaner worked. *This lad is going to make a very good fireman if he continues in this vein. I'll make sure Sid knows that.*

When they booked off in Chester again later that day, George went straight home and Lance also turned to leave for home but found his way blocked by John Fletcher, with an angry face.

"You got me into trouble with my bloody driver, yer little shit!" he snarled. "Yer goin' ter get yer face smacked for that!"

Lance was surprised; violence was rare in this shed, their foreman saw to that. Sidney Thomson fined all participants heavily without asking any questions.

Lance stared back. "An' oo's goin' ter smack me face?"

"I am!" growled Fletcher. "As soon as yer get out an' inter St Anne Street." He turned and walked off.

John Fletcher was a good two inches taller than Lance and known for a fondness for using his fists, but Lance had a stocky build and decided that he would accept the challenge. He suspected that Fletcher used both his size and his aggressive attitude to cow others but wasn't as good at fighting as he thought he was.

"I s'pose I'm goin' ter find out soon," Lance muttered to himself as he walked up St Anne Street and saw Fletcher waiting near a small side street.

"In 'ere," Fletcher pointed into the quiet street and walked in with Lance following.

"You're goin' ter learn a bit o' respect, Hargreaves," said Fletcher, turning to Lance and lifting his fists.

"Why?" demanded Lance.

"I told yer, yer got me inter trouble!"

"No, I didn't. That weren't me, yer got yerself inter trouble by not doin' yer job," countered Lance. "I didn't ferget ter 'ook yer couplin' up. Yer're just too bloody idle to do it yerself."

"Yer bastard!" Fletcher shouted and swung a fist at Lance's face.

Lance ducked and the blow missed, and when Fletcher turned back to him, Lance punched him hard in the stomach. Fletcher grunted and bent down in pain and Lance lifted his knee, which collected Fletcher on the chin. Fletcher groaned and fell.

Lance grabbed him and pulled him up again. "Next time, think agen before yer try to 'it someone!" he said with a grin, "Yer all piss an' wind!" And he walked off, rubbing his skinned knuckles.

After three months and several runs with Passed Cleaner Hargreaves, George had decided that the young man was one of the most promising mates he had ever worked with.

"He's intuitive in the work, Sid; somehow he automatically does things he's not learned," George told the shed foreman. "If we're careful with him, one day he will make a driver we can be proud of. He's very much at home in a cab."

"Yes George, other enginemen have said much the same. He needs to curb his inclination to be a bit bolshy at times, and he'll have to tone down his language if he wants to get ahead. I doubt that we can do much about his lechery though."

George shook his head. "You're right there, Sid. The only person who can do anything about that is Hargreaves himself." He thought for a moment, then remarked with a grin, "Or some girl's angry boyfriend!"

Both men laughed.

***

One morning in late autumn, the phone rang in Sidney Thomson's office. He picked it up, listened for a minute, then said, "Yes, I'll do that, Jack, but you'll owe me one!"

Swearing softly to himself as he put the phone down, he altered the duty roster for the following day and took it to the enginemen's messroom, where he pinned it up. Two or three enginemen walked up to peruse it and then went back to their card game, having noted the details without comment. Shortly after, Driver Denton walked in to see the duty board, smiled, and walked out again to find his fireman.

Lance was still hosing down the cab of their Pannier tank and looked up to see the smile on his driver's face. "Good news, Mr D?"

"Easy work for us tomorrow, Lance," George explained, "I'm on the cushions to Wrexham at 7.30 and then we'll be on shunting duty in Wrexham yard. They're a crew and an engine short; one of their engines came off the road injuring the crew. Nobody's seriously hurt, but they were able to drag the engine back onto the track and minor damage has been repaired already. We're part of a replacement crew."

"Sounds like an interestin' day and then we c'n 'ave— 'Ang on, you said '*I'm* on the cushions', not 'we're on the cushions'. Wot about me, then? Don't I get a nice comfy seat next to you in a coach?" Lance's face showed his indignation, but he wasn't game to express this to his driver.

"No, Lance. You get an interesting experience! We're both on the 7.30 to Wrexham this morning, but it's only me on the cushions. You're on observation in the cab."

"That's an auto train? With me in the cab?" An auto train was a small tank engine with a special coach for local services. When it reversed, the driver went to the front of the coach and drove from there, giving the fireman instructions via a whistle code and a link to the regulator lever in the engine's cab. Such a train needed a fireman with experience, who knew what they were doing.

"Right. You'll be in the engine's cab, Lance, so that you can see what the fireman does and how he gets his instructions from the driver." George grinned. "But at least you can sit down on the driver's seat because he'll be in the driving cab of the coach."

"Cor!" Lance didn't know how else to express himself; this was going to be a fascinating day; a completely new experience for him. Gradually, his face cleared. He was going to observe but not actually do any shovelling for a whole half-hour up the bank to Wrexham!

They were waiting on Platform 2 as the auto train moved in from the siding and passengers began to board. George climbed into the coach and Lance climbed into the cab, to introduce himself to the fireman. It felt quite strange to see only one man in the cab of the little tank engine – an 0-4-2T.

The regulator lever was attached to a link connecting it through the train to the front cab of the coach, where the driver sat. The platform starter signal dropped and the guard's whistle sounded. Lance watched, entranced, as the regulator gradually rose, seemingly by itself, the fireman released the engine brake, and the train began to move off.

The lightly loaded train gave the fireman plenty of breathing space on the short run to Wrexham. This was an easy duty, thought Lance, wondering whether he and his driver might one day find themselves on it for a week or two.

After they had passed Rossett up the bank, the fireman in the cab asked Lance what he thought of the duty.

"Looks easy enough, I s'pose," replied Lance, "why?"

"Think you could do it?"

"Yeah, I think so."

"Your driver wants you to have a bit more experience and he says a week doing this will help in promotion."

"Cor!" Lance couldn't think of anything else to say.

But their arrival in Wrexham drove such thoughts about possible promotion out of his mind. Their shunting engine was an elderly Pannier tan, which George was immediately displeased about, although Lance couldn't see why.

"What's the problem, Mr D? Yer don't look too 'appy."

"I'm not, Lance. I drove this engine last year and I think it should have gone for repair long ago, or even to the scrapyard. I'm not surprised it came off the rails; I thought then that it didn't feel right. I even left a note for the yard foreman, warning him that something was wrong."

"Well, p'raps they've done summat to it?"

"Does that explain why it derailed a day back?"

"Oh – er, no, I s'pose not."

George ran his eye over the dials and gauges then peered into the firebox. "Hmm, seems well prepared at least. Right, let's get on with it."

They began their work detaching five vans from a waiting freight and replacing them with two empty open wagons. The five vans were then shunted into a siding, ready to be attached to another freight to Manchester an hour later. They would add them to that train when it arrived.

So the day went on until eight in the evening, just before they came off duty. As they were moving their engine back to its stabling siding across the main line it derailed, blocking the main down line.

"Bugger!" exclaimed George, while Lance stared in shock. He had never heard his driver swear before. "I bet that foreman didn't pay any attention to my note! Well, he has to now; we'll be holding up the down Birkenhead."

The foreman arrived at the scene within minutes. "What have you done, George? You're holding up the Birkenhead!"

George stared back at him. "I gave you a note last year warning you about this engine!"

"I remember that, and I sent the engine to Wolverhampton. They sent it back reporting there was nothing wrong with it. I've still got your note and the engine's derailed twice since then."

"If I were you then, I'd send it back to them with a copy of my note and details of both derailments. Ask them why an engine without fault causes two accidents."

"I'll do that," replied the foreman, "and I'll let Sidney know you are not at fault yourselves."

"Thank you."

The breakdown crane arrived within half an hour; it had fortunately already been in Saltney, attending to a problem there.

The crew had the Pannier rerailed and back in its stabling siding within ten minutes. George and Lance caught the late down Birkenhead express back, listening with great interest to the complaints and explanations of other passengers as to why the train was late: a criminal had been arrested at Wrexham Station; the guard had been taken ill; a passenger had pulled the communication cord; the train driver was incompetent; all expressed with conviction.

These and similarly inaccurate explanations kept George and Lance highly entertained until they reached Chester and home.

11 - Beginner's Luck?
(June 1940)

Driver Barry Wilson drew slowly into Dover Marine Station with a motley collection of coaches hastily marshalled behind the Schools class 4-4-0 locomotive. The platform was thronged with soldiers, mostly in tattered uniforms, standing drinking mugs of tea or chomping greedily on buns and sausage rolls handed out by ladies from the WVS. A battered cruiser had just docked and discharged its load of 600 or so troops from the hell of Dunkirk. At least a third of them were wounded, and Barry could see that many covered bodies were being carried to the temporary morgue set up nearby.

"Look at these poor bastards on the platform, Ned; half of them don't know whether they are coming or going," he said to his fireman. "They're just glad to be getting out of France!"

Fireman Edward Sefton looked up from his place on the tender where he had been shovelling coal forward. "I know 'ow they feel, Barry," he answered. "I felt much the same when I came back from Passchendaele with a blighty in '17. All we wanted was to get mended then 'ave a bit of peace and quiet for a month or two. Then," he added, "not 'ave go back to the bloody war!"

"You got lucky then?"

"Yeah, but two o' the bullets are still in me leg."

While they were talking, a platform inspector climbed into their cab. "You are signalled right through to Redhill, Driver."

"Yes, sir. Er – where after that do we take these poor bug- er – these troops – to?"

"I'm not certain yet; I'll let you know when I find out."

"Right, sir; we'll look after them."

It was clear that the authorities wanted their train out as soon as possible as another was moving out from a siding to take its place and remove more troops from the crowding in Dover to somewhere with more adequate resources to deal with them. The starting signal dropped, and Barry eased the heavily loaded train out of the station and onto the main line north-west.

"Did you see those other soldiers, Barry?" said Ned. "They were in a large group together and away from the rest."

"Yes, I saw them. Who were they? They didn't look British."

"No, they were French troops also rescued from the German army."

"I heard that the French pulled their best aircraft back and the Army fell apart."

"My cousin's an RAF pilot, an' he told us that some of the French fighter aircraft were as good as the Messerschmidts but there weren't enough of 'em, an' French command didn't want to lose 'em so pulled 'em back."

"What about the troops?"

"Bloody good fighters but some of their commanders wanted shootin'!"

"Bad as that?"

"Yeah, ses my cousin anyway."

"Well, let's get them out of reach of the Luftwaffe. Poor sods must be totally knackered."

The guard's whistle sounded and Barry took the train gently away; he didn't want to shake the weary passengers any more than necessary. Although the train was heavy, their Schools had no trouble taking it away. These engines, although only 4-4-0s, were said to be among the most powerful of their class in Europe. As they left, the Mogul 2-6-0 already was already easing its train of empty coaches back, ready to take over their place at the platform.

They were lucky; they had a fast run past Folkstone Central and through Ashford without stopping, but nearing Tonbridge Wilson felt the brakes touch and looked back along the train to see the guard's red flag waving. He pulled up at the station platform and sent Ned Sefton to see what was happening.

"Problem, Mr Walker?" Ned asked the guard, who was striding towards him.

"Yes, Ned. We need to stop and get a couple of fellows off the train and into a hospital quickly. They need urgent attention; in fact, I don't think one of them'll make it!" he added gravely.

There were several nurses and doctors already waiting for just such a situation, and they unloaded half a dozen soldiers wrapped in blankets on stretchers into ambulances parked outside the station; one of the stretchers was gently taken out to one side and its patient's face covered.

The train was signalled away again and there were no more interruptions until they reached Redhill. Another official clambered up to the cab and informed the enginemen that they were to carry on with their train to Reading, where they would receive instructions to return to Dover with their Schools class.

"Sounds like a lengthy shift, today, Mr Wilson," remarked Ned.

"Don't think of your poor arms, Ned," advised his driver. "Think of the overtime!"

"Good point!"

Again, the run to Reading was smooth, but instead of running into the Southern station, they were signalled into the larger Great Western station. Ned slipped down to uncouple the coaches and saw a GWR Hall class engine back onto them at the rear and a GW guard came over to speak to the Southern guard.

"Anything special to report?" he asked.

"No, I can't say there is," replied Guard Walker. "Where are you taking them to?"

"Only as far as Oxford. They will be distributed from there to various destinations, I think. But this lot-" he pointed to a train of GWR coaches on the main up line – "are ECS to Dover, and I'll put a pound to a penny you'll be taking them!"

"Ah, I see. Yes, we'd been warned we were going back. So, Empty Coaching Stock for more of the PBI to be taken to safety?"

"PBI? Who are they?"

"Poor Bloody Infantry; I was one of 'em in the last lot." Ned stared at the dozen GWR coaches again and began to grin widely.

"What's so funny?"

"There are no first-class coaches: the officers will have to share with their men for a change!" Ned cackled. "Do the sods good! Too damn uppity by far, some of 'em!" He returned to his cab and reported the probability to Driver Wilson.

"Yes, I saw those coaches and thought that we might be taking them to Dover," replied his driver. "I hope we get a decent run back there."

Within the hour, they were heading back towards Dover but only got as far as Tonbridge. Here, a King Arthur class 4-6-0 was waiting as they pulled into the station.

"Why are we stopping here? We're for Dover with this ECS," Barry Wilson called out to the waiting railway official on the platform.

"Change of duty, Driver. The Arthur's taking your empties to Dover. You are to take over a Three Bridges train from the failing Mogul; it's struggling in from Edenbridge; that's if it gets this far." He peered down the line to see if there was any sign of the train. "Ah! You're in luck: it's coming in now."

The Mogul slowed to a stop. A door in the first coach opened and a soldier limped out, holding a crutch which he used to walk to the front of the train.

"Hey soldier, you're supposed to stay in the train; we're taking you all for medical assessment and rest!" called the official.

"I'll get back in as soon as the guard blows his tooter," said the soldier; he was, judging by the single stripe on his arm, a lance-corporal, but he was unconcerned by the official's instruction. "I just want to see the fireman uncouple." He watched with interest as the Mogul's fireman uncoupled and then waited for the Schools to back on and for Ned to couple up.

"Tricky job?" he asked as Ned climbed back onto the platform.

Ned looked round. "Tricky? Not really when you know what you're doing. Why?"

"I was always interested in firing engines as a kid, but the family sent me to work at fourteen." The lance-corporal had a strong Welsh accent.

Ned looked at the his crutch. "What would you know about shovelling coal?"

The soldier laughed. "Before I joined the army, I spent five years down a coal mine!"

"But not with a crutch!"

"It's an optimist I am!" smiled the lance-corporal and turned to walk back to his compartment.

Here, he met the doctor, who upbraided him. "We're trying to get you fellows fixed up but if you undo our efforts, you're wasting our time!"

"Call it exercise, Doc," smiled the soldier and he went back to his seat.

"Incorrigible," muttered the doctor as he went on his way. Ned grinned, shook his head, and climbed back into the cab.

***

Lieutenant Reynolds R.A.M.C. came up to the lance-corporal's bed and sat down with a sorrowful expression. "You'll never walk again without your crutch, I'm afraid, Lance-Corporal Jones," he told his patient. "However, I have some good news: you won't be fighting again either and you are to be discharged from the army next month on the first of November."

Harry Jones nodded. "Thank you, sir, for your care and help over these past weeks. It's grateful I am." Privately he thought, *Daft bugger! How did he get his medical degree? I've been walking round the grounds here for the last fortnight without my crutch!*

Some months later, Harry limped to the shedmaster's office at Long Rock, half a mile from the station at Penzance, and knocked on the door, entering as he heard the call to come in.

Gordon Swenson looked up from his desk. "What can I do for you, young man?"

"I'd like to join the railway, sir."

"Join the railway? As what?" Gordon was startled. *Why isn't this lad in the army?*

"I'd like to fire an engine, sir."

Gorden started to laugh. "A fireman has to serve years as a cleaner first! And anyway, how the hell have you avoided the army?"

Harry produced his discharge papers. "I've done my fighting, sir. Wounded at Dunkirk and discharged as unfit for military duty."

"I see," said Gordon, checking the papers carefully. "But you're limping; how can you fire a locomotive?"

"The medics told me I'd never walk again without a crutch, sir; but here I am."

Gordon sat back, thinking. *His papers are genuine, and he*

looks fit enough for general work around the place, and we're badly short of staff. He nodded slowly. "I can't help you with enginemen's work, but we could certainly use an extra hand. I'll give you a month's trial."

Eighteen months on, Harry was firing in the cab of a small prairie 44xx locomotive leaving Lelant for St Ives. Pre-war holiday makers had been the predominant passengers on this line, but numbers had dropped considerably since 1939. Henry had worked hard and learned quickly to overcome his injuries; so much so that he was by now classified as a Passed Cleaner and was allowed to fire under instruction. Gordon had seen his ability and pulled a few strings to get him into a cab on a route where, it was felt, he could gain experience with relative safety to the travelling public.

Driver Gerald Arbuthnot was an experienced driver who had been retained after his retirement date for the duration of the war. He watched as Harry shovelled coal, after checking where it was to go.

"You handle that coal well for a beginner," he remarked.

"I was a coal miner from the age of fourteen, Mr Arbuthnot, and I would have stayed one had it not been for the war. I'm used to handling coal."

"I can see that," Gerald nodded his approval. "And you're watching the steam and pressure almost like an old hand!" Then, with a grin, he asked, "Can you change a gauge glass?"

"I think so."

Gerald leaned over with a spanner in his hand and smacked the gauge glass with it. Hot water shot out, but Harry grabbed his bag and pulled out a replacement glass and had it on inside three minutes.

Gerald nodded his appreciation; he had one ready in his hand as well. "Who taught you that?"

"One of the fitters; Bob, I think his name is. I asked him to show me and paid him with my old army boots!"

By this time, they were approaching St Ives and Harry opened the fire doors and checked the fire; he put one more shovelful of coal down the left-hand side and shut the doors again.

"That should do us until we need to start our return," he explained to Gerald.

They slowed down as they drew into the little terminus and Gerald shut off steam, eased the engine to a stop, and applied the brake. Harry left the cab to drop down and uncouple the locomotive, while Gerald watched surreptitiously with approval, as Henry undid the steam heating and vacuum pipes and lifted the heavy link off the coaches hook so that his driver could move forward from the coach. *This young fellow knows his onions*, he thought.

Gerald moved his engine slowly forward over the crossover then, after the switches clicked over, backed to pass the coaches until he could run forward over the other crossover at the station approach to couple up to the other end of the train ready for their return. They had almost an hour to wait until they were due to return to St Erth and had time for their sandwiches and tea.

Gerald enthralled Harry during the break by relating some of his experiences on the Plymouth expresses. Later, both men were beginning to ready the locomotive when they saw their guard returning to his van. It wasn't long before he whistled, the starter signal dropped into the 'clear', and Gerald released the brake and eased the train out of the platform and onto the single line ahead.

It was after they had just crossed the viaduct outside St Ives that Harry caught a brief glimpse of a plane, but it disappeared past the cab roof before he could see it clearly.

"Is there a problem with enemy aircraft round here, Mr Arbuthnot?" he asked. "I think I just saw an aircraft."

"Not often, Harry, but there's an RAF station at St Eval with fighters because we have had an occasional bombing raid, but they've always been at night so far. With Spitfires and Hurricanes here, the daylight attacks are too dangerous for the buggers."

"Makes me feel easier!" chuckled Harry "I saw enough of them while hanging around at Dunkirk."

There were a few passengers at Carbis Bay, and Harry took the opportunity to have a good look at the sky but saw nothing to arouse his concern. But as they were approaching St Erth a few minutes later, he saw a bomber flying low across their path, one of its engines burning fiercely.

"A burning Heinkel coming in to crash-land in front of us!" he yelled urgently.

"What? Where?" Gerald stared out over the bunker. The bomber came lower, right over the railway, crashed into a field, and continued burning 300 yards away from them, scattering large and small pieces of wreckage in all directions.

Instantly, Gerald grabbed the emergency brake and shut off steam to bring the train to a sudden stop. They were just in time: a large metal wing frame had landed across the track, and it would have certainly derailed the train.

"Bloody hell, Harry, thank God you saw that plane crashing! Without your warning we would have run into that piece of wreckage!" Gerald was still shaking as he spoke.

"Shall I let the guard know? He might not have seen why we stopped in the emergency."

"Yes, he'll need to check the passengers too; lucky we don't have many. Then you'll need to warn the signalman, although he must have seen the crash."

Within ten minutes, police and ambulances had arrived from nearby St Erth and were checking the passengers for injuries. Four or five men hoping for souvenirs were being chivvied away from the burning aircraft by police.

"Get out of here, you daft buggers!" roared the police sergeant. "There'll be exploding ammunition!" This had not occurred to them, and they raced away.

"Pity an exploding round didn't hit that bastard with the cap," muttered the sergeant to Gerald and Harry as he watched the men hurry off, "he's been a bloody menace round here for years, but we've never been able to nail the sod!"

"The passengers will have to wait for bus transport into St Erth," said Gerald to Harry, "and we'll have to wait until we're cleared to move as well, after they clear that wreckage from the track."

The following Saturday, Gerald and Harry were called into divisional headquarters in Newton Abbot, where they were awarded commendations for their quick action by the Chief Divisional Officer himself. On their return to duty, they had to change trains at Plymouth and were waiting there when a Southern Railway train pulled in and came to a stop, just where they were waiting for their own connection to Penzance.

The Southern fireman saw them and stared at Harry, frowning.

"I've seen that bloke before somewhere, Barry," he said to his driver, "Can't think where though."

"Nip out and ask him, Ned; we've got a seven-minute stop here."

Ned slipped out and walked up to the waiting enginemen. "I've seen you before," he said to Harry, "but I can't recall where."

Harry stared back for a moment then smiled. "Tonbridge, it was: I was watching you uncouple your train, and we chatted for a minute or two. But that would've been almost two years ago now."

Ned's eyes widened. "You were that army lance-corporal I spoke to!"

"That's me!"

Gerald stepped in to add, "He's now a GWR passed cleaner with a commendation! He warned me to stop our train before it hit some wreckage on the line."

"Blimey! Well done, mate, well done!" Ned held out his hand.

"Not really. It was beginner's luck, look you, just beginner's luck!"

12 - There's no Safety at Home
(April 1941)

During the Easter holiday there was the usual group of young schoolboys gathered on the platform at Oxford Station, recording the numbers of the engines they saw moving through. At this juncture of the war, Oxford was very busy and locomotives from all four major companies could frequently be seen. SR, LMS and even LNER engines made regular appearances on through trains to and from the north and south, even though Oxford was firmly on the GWR. The LMS had a small station at Rewley Road next door to the GWR station; it was a local route serving Bletchley and Cambridge and the route was occasionally used for LMS locomotive trials.

"Hey! Here's another Southern engine! Cor, what a whopper!"

The call came from a youngster at the end of the main up platform as he caught sight of a train of Southern coaches hauled by a large and peculiar-looking flat-sided Pacific locomotive which stopped at the opposite platform. The engine uncoupled and moved off as a GWR Castle backed on.

"It's one o' them 'normouse Merchant Navy jobs!" shouted another lad. "I 'aven't seen one o' them before!" And he excitedly noted its number in a little notebook. As he spoke, another train pulled in on their own platform, hauled by a GWR Grange class engine. It stopped close to them, and one boy peered at the front of the engine, remarking, "Yer don't see one o' them 'ere too often."

"A Grange, Smithy?" mocked another. "Common as muck here!"

"Not this one," responded Smithy with a smug look on his face. "It's a Chester engine; they don't often get this far."

"'Ow d'yer know it's from Chester?" demanded his mate. "It's not like an LMS engine with its shed number on the smokebox."

Smithy crooked his finger. "Look 'ere," he said, pointing to a spot under the framing in front of the cylinder. The second boy looked carefully. "Oh yeah: CHR, I never knew that."

The other boys also stared at it. "Blimey!" said one. "Do all GWR engines 'ave their shed codes there?"

"Most of 'em," replied Smithy in lofty pride, "but yer can't always read 'em if the engine's grubby."

"What they usually are these days," remarked another.

"Why can't they keep 'em clean, like they used to?" complained another.

"Don't be daft! Don't yer know there's a war on? They 'aven't got enough men to clean 'em; they've all gone to fight."

"Not jus' men," called another lad. "I was walkin' past the shed las' week an' I saw a woman cleanin'!"

"A woman?" scoffed another.

"Yep. She 'ad a scarf on 'er 'ead, an' she 'ad them lumps on 'er chest!"

A slow freight loaded with tanks clanked past, heading south on the through line with a grimy Mogul at the head. All boys peered at the front cylinder.

"RDG," read Smithy. "Easy: that's Reading!"

Another Mogul steamed past northwards, with fish vans. They all gazed at the locomotive's front cylinder.

"SRD? Alright, Mr Knowitall; where the 'ell's that from?" one lad demanded, staring at Smithy.

Smithy grinned, "It's a long way from 'ome."

"Yeah, but where's 'ome?"

"I know!" claimed another. "It's from somewhere with bad engines."

"Bad engines?" Smithy was puzzled.

"O' course: SRD is the code fer 'Soddin' Rotten Depot'?"

Most of the boys hooted with laughter; they often resented Smithy's omniscient attitude.

"Stafford Road, Wolver'ampton, yer stupid bugger!" snarled Smithy, annoyed that his superior knowledge had been ridiculed. He snapped his notebook shut and stalked off.

"Good riddance ter bad rubbish!" shouted one of the boys after Smithy, who simply gesticulated with his upright finger without turning round.

On the arriving Grange, Lance Hargreaves grinned at Driver George Denton as they moved gently away from their coaches so that a Southern engine could back on to take the train further to the south coast. He pointed to the group of boys. "I dunno 'ow many hours I spent doin' that, Mr D," he said. "We was often at the end o' Platform Four in Chester, an' sometimes standin' on the 'oole Lane bridge watchin' the LMS engines comin' an' goin' from their shed. Me mum 'ad given me sandwiches an' tuppence fer buyin' a bun or a drink."

Driver George Denton's eyes twinkled. "So, you were keen on trains before girls then, Lance, were you?"

"Nah, trains were me day's fun; girls was fer the evenin'!"

George chuckled, shaking his head. *The lad always has the last word!*

The starter signal dropped and they moved slowly away to Oxford shed for turning and servicing for their return shift the following day. They were to stay overnight at the railway hostel accommodation; then they would pick up the coaches arriving at Oxford from the south coast and relieve the Southern engine to take the train on to Chester, where they would come off duty. Three or four coaches would also be taken off and the remaining six or seven would then continue with another crew the last few miles to Birkenhead. Those remaining at Chester would be added to the return train the next day.

At the shed early that evening, Lance got chatting to Roly Henderson, fireman of a local stopper to Princes Risborough.

"'Ow d'yer like workin' in London, Roly?" he began. "With all them bombs?"

The fireman shrugged his shoulders. "It's where I live, Lance, and any'ow yer get used ter the bombin'; nuthin yer c'n do about it."

"Rather you than me then."

"Where d'you work?"

"We're in Chester."

"Quiet up there, is it?"

"Yeah, but Birken'ead's not quiet, nor Brum."

"Well, you must be used ter the bombin' then an all."

Lance grinned at him. "It's where I live an' there's nuthin' yer c'n do about it."

Both men burst out laughing.

"Fer a young'un, ye're a cheeky bugger!" grinned Roly.

"That's wot me boss often ses."

Roly roared with laughter, "Yes, I bet he does! I just 'ope yer don't meet a driver wot don't 'ave your sense o' 'umour, Lance. Ye'r'll be askin' fer trouble!"

Fireman Henderson took his leave and left to climb into the cab of a big Prairie 2-6-2 which moved off shed to pick up its train of non-corridors for the run to Marylebone. His driver, Jack Emsworth, called out, "Where've you been, Roly?"

"Just yackin' to a fireman, Jack."

"What's he had to say for himself?"

"'E ses 'e's from Chester up north somewhere."

"Oh, yeah? I've been up there once; nice quiet city – no bombing, I've heard."

"They work up to Birken'ead an' Brum, though. Not as quiet as yer'd think."

"And here's me thinking we had all the fun!"

As they were chatting, both were busy preparing their locomotive. But just as they had finished, a fitter came and called up, "Jack, the boss ses yer'll 'ave twenty minutes' wait before yer c'n be cleared for the station. Problem with the signal lamp; the electrician's up there now fixin' it."

"Righto, ta." Jack looked at Roly. "Sounds like we'll have time for a quick brew, Roly. Get the can in."

Roly nodded, picked up their tea can and climbed down to fill it with fresh water from a nearby tap. Most enginemen much preferred fresh water over boiler water if they could get it.

"Wonder if we'll get another raid tonight," mused Jack as he slurped his tea. "After the RAF belted them six months back and stopped the invasion, they're coming over at night to soften us up again."

"But some of 'em aren't gettin' back," Roly responded with a grin. "I saw one comin' down on fire; blew up over Acton."

A shout came from below, "Ye're clear ter go now, Jack!"

"Righto!" Jack shouted down into the darkness. "Let's be off, Roly."

Both men immediately packed the tea bags away and set about their work, Jack on the regulator and Roly checking that the fire was satisfactory, and they moved off. They left Oxford forty minutes late, just before eight in the evening and well into the dark. They tried to make up some of the lost time, but freight traffic was heavy, and they were held up twice, reaching Thame an hour late. Here they had to wait longer as there was an air-raid siren, but the 'all clear' sounded after seven minutes.

"Bombers for somewhere passing overhead, I shouldn't wonder," commented Jack.

But just before they reached Bledlow, a huge flash lit up the sky in front of them, accompanied by a monstrous explosion of noise. Instantly, Jack dropped the regulator and set the locomotive's brake, bringing the train to a shuddering stop.

"That looked like a bomb on or near the line ahead!" shouted Jack. "Nip out, Roly, and have a look!"

Roly did as instructed but was back again in five minutes. "Yes, you were right, Jack. The bomb has blown a crater in a field close to the track, and the main up line is skewed. We'd have run right into it and derailed or worse! The police and fire brigade from Risborough are there already. We're going to be stuck for a while."

In the meantime, Guard Alan Rigby had walked along the track, calling out to warn the passengers that there would be a delay due to enemy activity and answering that the track ahead might be damaged but that buses would be made available to ferry them to Princes Risborough, where they could seek further assistance.

A Permanent Way Inspector arrived, and his investigation showed that both tracks would need to be re-laid; a procedure which might take two or three days.

"You're cleared to back to Towersey, Driver," he told Jack, "and wait there for further instructions."

"Christ, Jack, I'm still quivering!" said Roly, looking at his shaking hands, "A minute earlier and that damn bomb could have blown us to Hell!"

"You and me both!" replied Jack. "I think we can count that

as our ration of fun for the month!"

The guard had chivvied all those few remaining passengers who had climbed out to see what was to be seen back into their seats and let Jack know that they could slowly back to the little halt at Towersey when he was ready. A 'wrong line' working form had been obtained from the signal bobby who had been apprised of the situation, and who would have had to have been blind not to see to explosion. He had phoned a warning up and down the line immediately.

Reaching Towersey, Jack stopped the train and Roly climbed down to uncouple the coaches. Jack moved the engine forward and then, as the points of the crossover changed, he backed on the down line to pass his coaches before pausing after the second crossover and moving forward again to where Jimmy was waiting to couple up for their unexpected return to Oxford.

Their shedmaster there greeted them. "Didn't expect to see you two back so soon," he grinned. "You're lucky I haven't got any more work for you, and you can both go home early!"

"Us lucky?" Jack shook his head in mock horror. "We nearly got blown to smithereens!"

"Yes, but you didn't, did you? And you got to get home a quarter of an hour early. What are you complaining about?"

"Come on, Roly, we'll get no sympathy here!" said Jack loudly as they left the shedmaster's chuckling presence.

***

Three weeks later, further west at Newton Abbot, Driver Alexander Hawkins and Fireman Michael Bellamy were preparing their van train for departure. They had a Hall class general-purpose 4-6-0 locomotive; a class that normally found approval with enginemen because of the remarkably wide range of duties it was capable of. It was rumoured that William Stanier, the LMS chief mechanical engineer, who had been involved with the production of the Halls before he was snapped up from the GWR, had used this class as a basis for his highly successful LMS Black Fives, also a general-purpose 4-6-0 locomotive.

"I'll be glad to get away from Newton this evening, Alec," remarked Fireman Bellamy, sipping his tea as they waited in the enginemen's mess. "What's our duty today?"

"Van train of empties for the West Country, Mick, dropping them off at Liskeard, Bodmin Road, Truro and so on through to Penzance."

"Nice, quiet run if a bit slow. What've we got to pull 'em?"

"A Hall just out of the workshop here; should be a good run. For a change."

"A newly repaired engine, eh? That's great! We don't get that every day!" Mick rubbed his hands in glee. "So, we're running it back in, so to speak?"

"Yes, I suppose so."

Alec picked his watch out of his waistcoat and looked at it. "Right, let's get to the steed."

They would need at least three quarters of an hour to prepare the locomotive for duty. In the dim light of the shed they could see that their Hall had been cleaned although not freshly painted; such luxuries had long been abandoned since many general staff had been called up. They worked together on their engine for an hour and then moved it outside to pick up their van train, before taking it slowly to the siding, ready to move onto the main down line when signalled to do so.

Newton Abbot was a large railway centre, once the headquarters of the South Devon Railway before it had been merged with the GWR in the previous century. It still had a large workshop capable of major repairs and clearly well worth the attention of the Luftwaffe. This evening Newton Abbot was to experience one of their visits.

Alec checked once more that the tarpaulin over the gap between the cab roof and tender was tight, limiting the chance of the light from the fire being seen from the sky, when suddenly the air-raid sirens sounded urgently. It was a sneak attack by a low-flying bomber which must have flown in under the radar. Two bombs landed nearby, doing little damage apart from smashing a coal wagon, spilling its load over the adjoining tracks. The plane soared quickly away before the anti-aircraft guns could focus on it.

"Lucky there was no serious damage done; that bomber caught everyone by surprise. I'll be bloody glad to get into quiet Cornwall!" gasped Alec.

After the bomber had left and the 'All Clear' had sounded, all was quiet for half an hour while the two men waited with their train for their route to be cleared to leave the yard and head off over the Devon banks. They had no qualms about the next section to Plymouth; heavy West Country expresses often had to stop at Newton Abbot to pick up a pilot engine, and even the mighty Kings were not permitted to take more than 360 tons unaided over the banks. Most other expresses from London picked up a Hall or a Grange to help them up past Brent. But their empty van train was relatively light and should be no problem for a Hall in – presumably – good nick after repairs.

But that single bomber had presaged a heavier attack, and the air-raid warning sounded again just as their signal dropped, indicating they were cleared for departure.

"Now what, Alec? Shall we clear off quick and get away? Or should we head for the shelter?" Mick was gazing avidly into the sky.

Alec thought for two seconds. "No, let's bugger off quick; the enemy haven't arrived yet. We may have fifteen more minutes; enough to get us well away from the yard here, if we get our skates on."

They did not hesitate.

"With any luck, we'll be out of the danger zone very soon." Alec was trying to pick up speed as quickly as he dared with the train, while Mick stared out of the cab, trying to see where any bombs might be coming down. The first were already dropping but they were off target out in the river, and a second pair landed further south, near Netherton.

The third strike was directly on target. One bomb fell on the middle vans of their train, throwing the guard off his feet in his van and breaking both his legs. Four of the empty vans were completely destroyed and three more were derailed and badly damaged. The second bomb fell right beside the locomotive, blowing it off the rails and shattering the boiler and cab. Both Driver Hawkins and Fireman Bellamy were killed instantly. The

0-6-0 Pannier tank on the adjacent track was also blown onto its side, and its four wagons were turned into matchwood, but fortunately the Pannier had been unoccupied because the driver and fireman had run for the shelter as soon as they had heard the sirens. Several more bombs fell on the yard and workshop and, although no more staff were killed, fourteen suffered injuries of varying degrees, from serious to minor. All the injured were taken by ambulance but nothing could be done for the two enginemen.

In the daylight next morning, the extent of the damage was clear: it was going to take days before the wrecked vehicles could be removed and scrapped and the tracks repaired. The workshop damage was more serious and it would be weeks before it could be brought back into full operation again. It was fortunate that the station and main line through the town were not hit, and traffic between Paddington and Devon and Cornwall would not be badly affected, although some traffic would need to be diverted through the Southern main line as far as Plymouth. This was occasionally done with the co-operation of the Southern Railway when track damage from the sea storm surges closed the line at Dawlish. It wasn't common but both railway companies were prepared for it.

The Hall class engine was lifted and taken away and covered by a tarpaulin, away from public view until it could be assessed for either repair or scrapping. In the case of a seriously damaged boiler, engine repair was usually deemed impractical, and the engine was scrapped.

In Newton Abbot, a funeral was held a week later and was attended by most non-duty staff. Alec Hawkins and Mick Bellamy had been popular.

As the congregation drifted away, one railwayman grumbled to his mate, "The public are always sorry for the blokes we lose in the fighting, but they complain bitterly about poor railway service and don't bloody realise why!"

13 - Lance Shirks a Duty
(Nov 1941)

Driver James Hardy groaned as they steamed slowly across the points into a siding just outside Wrexham on the LNER line to the north.

"I bet we're here for a lengthy spell again, Jake," he grumbled. "Our coal for Birkenhead docks is important but not urgent, so we have to wait for the regular passenger trains. That wouldn't be so much of a problem if we'd only been on duty for eight hours, but we're doing Chester to Manchester and back, and then south to Wrexham for a Birkenhead and back on a freight duty!"

"Yeah, and it only needs some officious bugger to say, 'Don't you know there's a war on?' for me to smack him one on the conk," Fireman Jacob Smith replied, shovelling carefully after checking in the firebox where the coal was most needed.

James Hardy grinned. "I'd like to see that, Jake, I really would; it would make life worth living again!"

"It would make me feel much better too."

"I doubt that, Jake; you'd get the sack and have to join the army and get shot at by the Jerries! Now, let's make the best of it and have a wet." Driver Hardy's optimistic nature came briefly to the fore.

"You've got really good ideas sometimes, Jim! I'll get the water on while you dig out the tea and milk."

"An early breakfast would be a good idea too, if we hadn't eaten our sandwiches already," grumbled Hardy, checking his watch in the firelight to find that it was still only 5am.

"I wonder if Merseyside caught a packet again in the night," said Jake. It was quite likely; Merseyside docks had been getting plenty of attention from the Luftwaffe recently. The matter was confirmed as he spoke: they heard a *ratatat!* in the sky above them as an unseen fighter attacked a German bomber that was presumably trying to journey home. There was returning fire from the bomber and both aircraft flew on until the sound faded.

The train was kept in the siding until a passenger train for Chester passed and their signal changed to clear, and the points clicked over to allow them out onto the main line. Their Robinson ex-Great Central 2-8-0 freight engine moved out easily and gently and they settled down to take their coal train north. Later, they crossed the River Dee and passed the junction where the two main lines diverged, one to Chester and the other on to Birkenhead docks.

These Robinson 2-8-0s had been the mainstay of freight traffic for the Great Central Railway and had been both strong and reliable. They had also been chosen as the standard freight engines of the Railway Operating Division and more than 500 had been built for work during the First World War. Even the Great Western, with its far superior 2-8-0s, had picked up a hundred of them after the war, for one hundred pounds each as war surplus, although GWR men did not much like working on them.

The two men were able to pick up more speed and dawn began slowly to break, the track ahead steadily revealing itself. But out of nowhere, Hardy's horrified shout alerted his fireman as the driver pointed to the sky. Another Luftwaffe bomber was flying towards them with two RAF fighters attacking it, one from either side. The bomber, however, was giving as good as it was getting, and one of the fighters veered away, apparently out of control. Its left engine suddenly began to spit out flames as the second fighter fired another burst. The other fighter pilot had clearly regained control of his plane and returned to the attack, which appeared to succeed as the bomber simply exploded in a flaming ball and aircraft wreckage began falling from the sky; well to the right of the railway, to the relief of the two enginemen.

"Thank God for that!" muttered Jake, shaking. "I thought we were goners then, Jim."

Hardy nodded his vigorous agreement. "So did I, Jake. Until that second plane attacked, I feared we'd be getting either a bomb or a crashed plane on our skulls!"

"I bet those two fighters were from RAF Hooton, but that bomber can't have been from Merseyside; any from there would have been gone long ago. I bet it was coming back from Belfast and perhaps got lost on the way home."

As they were speaking, they passed the site of burning wreckage, half a mile away on their left.

"Better keep an eye open," muttered Driver Hardy to himself. "The bugger might have jettisoned a bomb or two on his way back."

This remark was prophetic. Jake, turning to the firebox with his shovel full of coal, caught a glimpse ahead a pall of smoke through the spectacle plate. He dropped the shovel. "Jim, there's smoke ahead of us!"

Driver Hardy instantly lowered the regulator and applied the engine's brake, whistling a warning to the guard to apply his brakes as well. Being an unfitted goods, the wagons' brakes could only be applied individually by someone running alongside and dropping each in turn, but the guard could help by braking his heavy van.

Both men saw the large smoking crater directly alongside the track 150 yards ahead. The train was perceptibly slowing but its weight was too much for the engine's brakes and the inertia pushed it inevitably forward. It was clear that they could not stop in time and Hardy shouted to his fireman, "Jake, jump for your life!"

Jake leapt out of the cab and hit the ground, rolling over several times before standing up to watch the train grinding forward until the locomotive tipped sideways and slid into the crater, followed by half a dozen coal wagons, before the rest came to a standstill.

Jake raced over to the crater where he met the Goods Guard Johnson and, both severely shaken, hurried to see if Driver Hardy had managed to get out in time. Inside the crater, the tender was sitting on top of the locomotive's cab. There was steam hissing from the cylinders and a wisp of smoke emanating from the chimney, but no sign of life from the cab.

"Is it safe to climb in, d'you think, Mr Johnson?" Jake asked.

Johnson looked around the crater, examining the positions of the tender and the wagons, before nodding and saying, "I think so, but I want you to run and warn the signal bobby. We're due to pass another south-bound train in four minutes. If the signalman doesn't know about the crater, we could lose many lives! Now quick, get going!"

Jake nodded and ran off to the nearest signal box. The signalman there would phone through a warning up and down the line, and this would also fetch the emergency services, if they hadn't already been notified by anyone else.

Ferdy Johnson slid cautiously down the crater until he could grab the engine's buffer beam, which gave him enough purchase to climb up and work his way along the footplate. A sudden shift of the huge tender above gave him a bad fright, but nothing else moved and he continued until he could see into the cab. Jim Hardy was lying up against the slanting firebox, not moving, and when Johnson moved closer, he saw why. A tender wheel had broken off its axle and had sliced deeply into the unfortunate driver, almost cutting his chest in half.

Johnson looked away and tried to prevent himself from vomiting at the sight. He waited until he could control himself once more and began working himself back and out of the crater.

"Give us your hand, mate!" called the dark figure above him as he reached the edge; he was hauled to safety by a powerful police constable

"You alright?" asked the policeman.

"Yes, I think so. The driver's dead though. His body's still in the cab."

"You sure he's dead?"

"Oh yes. A tender wheel has almost cut him in half; gallons of blood everywhere." Johnson was shaking and the constable grabbed quickly him to prevent him falling back into the crater.

"I think you need attention too, sir," said the constable, "We've a doctor here. I'll get him to look at you."

"No need, thanks Officer, I'm fine now."

"Pardon me, sir, but you're clearly not. You're still shaking. Are there any more men we should be looking for?"

"No; I sent the fireman to the signal box to warn the bobby."

"Bobby? Which bobby?" asked the constable, looking around for a fellow officer, puzzled.

"Sorry; we call our signalmen bobbies."

The doctor arrived, looked at Johnson, and took his thermometer out. "Open wide," he said and pushed the thermometer under Johnson's tongue, then took it out and looked at it.

"Hmm," he muttered.

"I'm really alright," protested Johnson.

"Are you arguing with me? I'm a professional!" replied the doctor sharply. "You're in shock; I prescribe a small brandy, and luckily, I have one."

He produced a little pocket flask, poured a small measure into it and thrust it at Johnson, who took it and swallowed.

"Thank you!" the guard said, handing the small cup back.

It took three days to clear the wreckage and another week before the crater could be filled again and the track re-laid.

***

The weather had changed and become very much more like winter, with a cold wind whistling round Driver Denton's and Passed Cleaner Hargreaves' legs as they walked into the enginemen's mess at Chester's GWR shed.

"Easy day, today, Lance," said George Denton to his fireman as they greeted the few men sipping their teas.

"What's fer us terday then, Mr D?"

"We run a local stopper as far as Ruabon, then back on the cushions and then we take an express to Stafford Road and then back with a return Birkenhead."

"So we're not workin' 'ard fer a change?"

"It would appear that way, Lance."

They walked to their Mogul 2-6-0 and spent an hour preparing it before moving off shed to the station and their train which had just arrived from Birkenhead behind a large 2-6-2T Prairie. They backed on and within ten minutes were on their way. Less than an hour later, in Ruabon, they were handing the engine over to a Croes Newydd crew from Wrexham, who took the train on to Pwyllheli.

The two enginemen waited on the platform for the stopping train back to Chester where they returned to the shed to take over their Star class 4-6-0 ready for the up Paddington. The Stars were seen originally as Churchward's masterpieces and had been among the finest express locomotives in the country; they were fast, and powerful, but many were over thirty years old. The Castles and then the Kings had both been developed directly from the Stars. Enginemen still liked them despite their age, and George was no exception.

"Could be a really good day today, Lance!" he remarked, smiling.

"Sounds interestin', Mr D." Without knowing it, Lance spoke prophetically.

The run to Wolverhampton was straightforward, with no surprises, but Lance enjoyed the section across the plain, picking up speed to tackle the rise into the hills before Wrexham and then the fast run through Baschurch to Shrewsbury. Their Star had just come out of the works at Wolverhampton and was in good condition, giving them a faultless run.

The return was quite different, however; their train from Paddington rolled in with a King at its head, then the King and the first five coaches uncoupled and moved off. George backed their Castle on and made ready to start. The guard's green flag rose and his whistle sounded and then the starter signal dropped, George eased the brake off, and they began to move.

This should have been easy with a Castle and only ten corridors, but the engine seemed to be making heavy weather of the job. George frowned: the regulator was stiff and needed to be forced a little, and the steam did not give the cylinders the pressure they needed, in spite of Lance's shovelling. However, they finally had the train moving at a respectable speed. The stop at Wellington gave Lance the chance to put more coal into the fire, and the stops at Shrewsbury, Gobowen, Ruabon and Wrexham all gave him short chances to rest, but they still reached Chester twenty minutes behind time.

As they were bringing the locomotive into the shed, shedmaster Sid Thomson was waiting for them.

"Problem, George?"

"Yes, Sid. Our Castle badly needs a 'sole and heel'; she's very tired!"

"I'll see what I can do. Now, talking of very tired, I'm afraid I've got an urgent duty for you both. And don't tell me you've already worked a full shift because I know that, and I'm sorry George, but I've been given direction from on high at Division and can't do anything else at the moment."

"What's the job, Sid?"

"It's a fast freight to Bristol, but you'll be relieved at Hereford and come back on the cushions. D'you think you can manage with young Hargreaves?"

"Yes, he'll grumble but he'll do it; he's a good lad." George walked off to find Lance and give him the good news.

"Another two hours, Mr D?" Lance was horrified. "I'm knackered already, and—" He tailed off unhappily.

"And? And what? Think of the overtime pay."

"Yeah, I s'pose so."

George stared at Lance for a moment then nodded, smiling. "And you've got some unfortunate girl lined up for this evening, haven't you?"

"'Ow did yer know?"

"I've been your driver for long enough. Now let's see what Sid's giving us for the job."

They had a Grange class 4-6-0, which pleased George. The Granges were much the same as Halls but their smaller 5'8" wheels gave them an edge on power over the Halls, which had 6' wheels. Like the Halls, the Granges could run if needed. They were popular with most enginemen, and their Grange was no exception. It had a mixed set of vans and wagons and was merely waiting for its crew. George and Lance climbed in and found everything prepared for them and in ten minutes they were off.

"I 'aven't been on one o' these Granges much," remarked Lance as they passed under the city walls, "but I like 'em."

"Yes, they are good and reliable engines," replied George, "and they are more forgiving than Halls."

But there was little conversation between the two men on the trip; both were tired and needed to concentrate on the job in hand.

They were signalled into Coleham Yard at Shrewsbury to add half a dozen vans before they were able to continue south on the line to Hereford.

"Gawd," said Lance, hiding a yawn as they slowed down due to a signal check, "I'll be glad ter see 'ereford an' 'ave summat to eat an' a kip!"

"Yes," replied George, "it's certainly been a longer day than we expected."

But both men were to be disappointed. The yard master at Hereford was waiting for them as they pulled in. He grabbed the handrail to climb into the cab.

"I don't like the look of this," muttered George quietly.

"I've got good news and bad news for you, Driver Denton."

George sighed. "I suspected that when I saw you climb in, sir. What's the bad news?"

"I am sorry to have to tell you that you are not being relieved here, you are to take the train on to Bristol. We have no spare crew at all, and the freight is needed there urgently."

"Always bloody urgent!" muttered Lance softly to himself. The yard master's eyes swivelled round to Lance. "What was that, Hargreaves?"

"Er – we don't need urgin', sir."

"And the good news, sir?" asked George quickly, to redirect the man's attention.

"Oh yes; you are both permitted to return from Bristol as passengers."

"Oh, goody!" murmured Lance quietly, and the eyes swivelled sharply round again, but Lance was staring vacantly out of the cab.

"You've got time for a quick brew, while we attach three more vans, and you can get on your way," added the yard master, "er – with our thanks."

George nodded, "Sir."

The man glanced suspiciously at Lance once more and climbed down. Lance grabbed their tea can and filled it with water from the boiler. Neither man enjoyed boiler water but fetching fresh water from the nearest tap might hold them up. Within seconds the tea was made, and swiftly drunk just before the shunter's call came to inform then that they were ready to depart. The signal dropped and they were off again. It was dark already and despite the tea both men were dog-tired, but long shifts had become the norm these days and overtime was only a minor compensation.

Half an hour after leaving Hereford, they were directed into a refuge siding.

"I thought we were urgent," grumbled George, in a tone which surprised Lance; his driver was usually more patient. An express passenger rattled past but their starter signal to allow them to move back onto the main line remained stubbornly at 'stop'.

"Can't even 'ave tea," muttered Lance, looking into his bag, "I've got none left." As he spoke, another passenger train hurried past.

"Must be something important to interrupt us," said George. "I can't see why they would keep us waiting otherwise."

He sat down on the driver's seat – or shelf, to be more accurate; it wasn't designed for comfort. Lance followed suit and used his seat; something he very rarely did.

More time passed and once or twice another train did too, as both men sat dozing quietly until George shook himself, sat up abruptly, and pulled out his watch, and saw that they had been sitting for almost an hour.

"Lance, how's the steam pressure?" he called over.

Lance shot up, annoyed he had dozed off. "Gawd, the fire!" he snapped and leapt to open the firebox: the fire was very low, and the steam pressure was right down. He quickly grabbed the pricker, raked the fire into life again, and threw four shovelfuls of coal into the dead spots; the fire quickened again, and Lance added a dozen more shovelfuls until pressure began to rise once more.

"I'm so sorry, Mr D," Lance was mortified. "I was so knackered, I nearly let the bloody fire out!"

"Not entirely your fault, Lance, lad; I should have noticed as well. In any case, there'll be nothing in my journal except that we had to wait for the signal."

After more coal went in, both men waited, hoping the signal

wouldn't drop until they had enough steam pressure to move. They were lucky; it had just reached 120psi when the signal clanged and they were able to move off. They arrived over an hour late in Bristol, having completed an eighteen-hour shift.

They quietly boarded a train for Shrewsbury, settled down in their seats, and promptly fell asleep, waking at Shrewsbury and changing onto a Chester local, arriving home over twenty-four hours later than planned.

"Oo'd be an engineman, comin' 'ome more'n a day late?" grumbled Lance as he arrived home.

"Look on the bright side, son; you could be in the army," replied his dad from his wheelchair, "and never get home at all!"

14 - Driver Smith and the Brigadier
(May 1944)

Marty Smith backed his engine, a Mogul 2-6-0, from its local goods from Wellington into Chester's GWR shed. His shift was over.

"Shorter shift today," he said, smiling at his fireman, sweeping the coal remnants from the cab floor. "Got a bird lined up?"

"Yep. She don't know how lucky she is," cackled Lance Hargreaves.

Marty had not had Lance as a mate before but had heard good reports of the lad and wanted to see for himself how he worked in a cab. Unfortunately their engine, like most other engines in the war, badly needed attention from the fitters but had yet to be serviced. It had become a question of 'Keep 'em running until they break down' in all four major railway companies; there were insufficient locomotives for all the duties required. Often it was only when engines actually broke down that they received the attention they needed; even then it was the minimum required to get them back into service.

Earlier that morning, Marty had been surprised to see from the duties board that his fireman was Lance Hargreaves, who was normally Driver Denton's fireman. He went into the enginemen's mess but Lance wasn't there, so he walked over to their locomotive; the Mogul standing just outside the shed. Lance was in the cab, checking the fire.

Marty climbed up.

"Why aren't you with George Denton today, Lance?" he asked.

"Mr D's got a problem with 'is gut an' 'as called in ter say 'e's unfit fer duty, today, Mr Smith."

"George Denton unfit for duty?" Marty was surprised. "I've never heard that before. George's one of the fittest men I know."

"I think 'e's eaten summat wot doesn't agree with 'im," said Lance. He too had never heard of George being sick and was worried it might be serious. He and Driver Denton had been together for most of the last few years and Lance couldn't imagine being paired with any other driver.

"Let's hope he's well again very soon," remarked Marty. Lance nodded his agreement.

"D'you know anything about this Mogul we've got today?"

"Not really, Mr Smith, but the firebox seems to be workin' 'unky dory, 's far's I c'n tell. Fire's burnin' well."

Their duty had taken them with an unfitted goods as far as Wellington, where they had exchanged with an Acton crew and taken the Acton goods north to Birkenhead, returning light engine to Chester, where they would book off-duty. However, the duty foreman told Marty that the shed foreman wanted to see him on his return.

In the office, Sidney Thomson asked him whether he could take on an extra duty. "We've something of an emergency, Marty. I've no other spare driver and we have been asked to supply an engine for an urgent army train from Crewe to Hereford. Crewe has nothing spare. You return with Hargreaves on the cushions."

"Our duty's been fairly easy, Mr Thomson," replied Marty. He was calculating the extra time needed: about four hours, yes, we could do that. "Lance is a fit lad, and I'm sure we could cope."

Twelve- and fourteen-hour shifts had become common for enginemen at this stage in the war. There was little point in complaining, and there was always the overtime pay anyway.

"Thank you. I'll let Crewe know and ask them to have some sandwiches ready for you and Hargreaves when you get there. I have a Castle ready for you now; it's been coaled and watered and is ready to leave."

Marty and Lance took the Castle light engine to Crewe, where they were to pick up a military special; he would receive further details there. They turned into the Crewe North shed to top up their coal and then backed into a refuge to wait for the military train to arrive from the north. A grinning porter arrived and climbed into the cab with a large bag. "You the starving Western men we have to feed before you take the army south?"

"Yeah, that's us," replied Marty. "Is LMS food edible?"

The porter's grin widened. "Dunno, this ain't ours, it's from the station canteen. It's 'orrible and only fit fer Great Western men."

"Odd that," remarked Lance. "In our GWR shed, we send our rubbish food to the LMS shed and they 'aven't complained yet!"

"No, I bet they aven't," agreed the porter. "My uncle's a driver there and 'e collects it all and gives it 'is pigs so 'e doesn't have ter buy pigswill!"

Marty laughed at the repartee, thanked the porter, and he and Lance made a start on the sandwiches, which were surprisingly tasty.

"Not often someone beats you to the punchline, Lance," commented Marty.

"Nah, I was distracted, wondrin' 'ow ter get me new bird ter, er – co-operate, like," explained Lance.

Just then an inspector mounted the cab.

"Thank you both for assisting us. The military train is running about forty-five minutes later than planned, so you've time for a brew-up and a toilet visit. There's been a cock-up, causing a change of route. You're to take the train as far as Birmingham Snow Hill, where a Reading crew will take over to take the train on to Southampton via Newbury."

"And how do we get back, sir?"

"On the cushions. This is an urgent job, Driver Smith, and you've been picked specially by your Sid Thomson. He tells me you're a good man in an emergency."

Marty was surprised to hear this; he had only been driving for a year, although he had once, while still a fireman, driven an ammunition train to Hooton with an unconscious driver. Firemen, even passed firemen, were not allowed to drive alone in a cab. Sidney Thomson had pointed out that Passed Fireman Smith had not actually been alone in the cab; his driver had been with him. Marty had passed his driver's test shortly after the incident.

Their train finally arrived, and Brigadier-General Montcalm was waiting for them at the platform when they backed their Castle on.

"I understand you men have been told this is a secret train and you are to assist us to get the men and equipment to Southampton as quickly as possible?"

"Er – no, sir," said Marty. "We were just told it was a military train."

"I see, well, our route is via Shrewsbury, Birmingham Snow Hill, Oxford, Newbury and Southampton, I am told. Will that be a problem?"

"Shouldn't be, sir."

"Excellent. Now you have a 300-ton train including a large van. I trust your engine can manage that?"

"Yes, sir."

However, the run to Shrewsbury was not as easy as they had expected. The locomotive was working hard.

"Anything wrong with the coal, Lance?" enquired Marty.

"Not really, Mr Smith, but the engine is greedy."

Marty frowned; that was his impression too. He gazed back along the train to see whether anything could explain their Castle's odd reluctance. It seemed longer than he'd expected but the guard had not mentioned anything. As they came into Shrewsbury, he stared again from the fireman's side as they rounded the sharp curve into the station. He wasn't able to count the coaches but he could clearly see two vans, not one, at the rear.

They pulled up at the platform to find an inspector waiting.

"You're four minutes down, Driver. Is there a problem?"

Marty frowned. "I don't know exactly, sir. She's not pulling as well as I expected, but I can't detect anything amiss with the engine, and my fireman says the coal's fine. The only thing I can think of is perhaps the weight of the train."

The inspector looked at the paper in his hand. "Three hundred tons, including a van, it says here."

"There's two vans, sir; you can see 'em at the rear."

Just then the guard came up. "Sorry, Driver," he gasped, "I didn't get a chance to see you in Crewe; that bloody brigadier is in charge and wouldn't hear of me 'wasting time' as he put it. 'Your driver has all the relevant details' he said to me."

"What's the train's weight?" asked Marty.

"It's 335 tons and two bogie vans, totalling almost three-seventy!"

"Ah," said Marty, "That explains our problem: we were told it was only 300!"

"Who told you that?" the startled inspector snapped at the guard.

"That brigadier, sir. And I'm not even sure that's right either. The carriages are packed; the squaddies are standing in the corridors. I'd guess it's nearer 400 tons."

"Four hundred tons?" gasped the inspector. "That's a job for a King; and Salop doesn't have any. No wonder you had problems! We can't even give you a pilot. I'm sorry Driver but you'll just have to manage as best you can."

"Snow Hill's not too far; I'm sure we can manage," said Marty optimistically.

"I'll have to warn Snow Hill; they'll need to have a King ready," the inspector muttered to himself as he left the cab.

Marty asked Lance to check for the guard's green flag while he was filling in the driver's journal but was surprised to hear his fireman's annoyed muttering.

"What's up?" he queried.

"As a fireman, I was once firin' an' we left 'ere fer 'ereford with nineteen coaches be'ind a 'all wiv no pilot!" he grumbled.

"A Hall with nineteen on and no pilot?" Marty couldn't believe it. "To Hereford?"

"Nah, we 'ad ter take the train ter Bristol! Geez, I was knackered after that; an' now they're doin' it ter me agen!"

"I'll give you a hand to Snow Hill," promised Marty. "I was firing myself only a year or so back."

"Ta, Mr Smith. We'll 'ave bin on duty fer – wot? Twelve hours?"

"It'll be thirteen by Snow Hill."

"Yeah, well I've 'ad worse."

The run to Snow Hill offered no difficulties and Marty gazed at the two Kings sitting cold on a siding as they passed Wolverhampton's Stafford Road shed. *We could do with one of those*, he mused with envy. *A King could handle over five hundred tons!*

But arriving in Birmingham's main up Platform in Snow Hill brought a further complication. No sooner had he applied the brake than there was a call from the platform. It was the brigadier once more. "For heaven's sake, man, must we stop all the damn time?"

Marty felt anger rising; he had had enough of this irritating man. "When a senior general gives you an order, do you question it every time?" he demanded.

"Of course not!" replied the brigadier, indignantly. "And neither would you."

"Exactly, sir. I too obey orders." Marty pointed to the end of the platform in front of them. "That's mine."

"What the hell are you talking about?"

"That's a signal and it orders me to stop. I cannot move until it shows clear. Now if you don't like it, you can complain to the Great Western Railway, the Army, or the bloody Ministry of War! Just don't come bellyaching to me and distracting me from my work." Marty stomped off to his side of the cab, leaving the brigadier spluttering with rage.

As the driver was cooling down, he noticed Lance unsuccessfully hiding a broad grin on his face, which he quickly hid as a locomotive inspector climbed into the cab.

"Driver Smith, I gather?"

"Yes, sir, that's me."

"The Army doesn't normally give us trouble, Smith, but today they've given us incorrect information and forgotten important instructions; as a result, we can't help them as we would like. How long have you been on duty?"

"About thirteen hours, sir."

The inspector sighed. "I was afraid of that. I'm sorry but we're having to ask you and your fireman to carry on to Oxford or possibly even Didcot. Can you do that with a degree of safety?"

Marty looked questioningly at Lance, who thought then nodded slowly.

"Yeah, I reckon we could, sir," Marty informed the inspector.

"Our grateful thanks to you both. At least we've found a pilot for you," he said, pointing as he left the cab. Waiting on the up main through line was a Grange.

"You're quite sure about the extra firing, Lance?" Marty was worried about his younger mate.

"Yeah, I'm thinkin' about me pay packet; it'll be the biggest I've ever 'ad!"

With another Grange as a pilot engine, they made easy work of the 400 tons, and they were signalled through Warwick, Leamington and Oxford without any further delay. Finally, they reached Didcot and pulled up to uncouple. An LMS 8F was waiting to take the train on through to Newbury and over the Berkshire Downs to Southampton.

As the relieved pair reached the platform, they found an important-looking group arguing ahead of them. The brigadier was one of the men and as soon as he saw Marty, he pointed him out to the others, calling, "There's the man responsible for most of the delay, sir; he's the driver!"

A general officer with red tabs came over, accompanied by two senior railway officials, one of whom snapped at Marty, "Are you responsible for the insolence given to this brigadier, Driver? If so, you will be severely reprimanded and must expect a loss of pay!"

The other official intervened: "Leave that for a moment, Geoffrey, there's a more important matter to be dealt with." He took Marty by the arm to one side. "We have a more important problem, Driver. The relieving driver of the 8F is not well. He claims he's fine, but his fireman tells me the man is not fit to drive. Can you take the train on to Southampton? The crew will be in the cab with you as you probably don't know the road, and your two firemen will make short work of the heavy firing over the hills. I wouldn't ask, but this train is urgent." He paused then added, "How long have you been on duty?"

"About fifteen hours, sir."

"Oh my god!"

"We'll give it a go, sir. Only another three hours and with two men in the cab who know the road and two firemen we should manage."

"Hmm," the official considered the matter. "Look, I'll pass you as far as Newbury and then I'll check again. I'll be in the first coach if any problem arises."

"Yessir, in a compartment with the brigadier?"

"Emphatically not."

"Sir." Marty turned away with a grin and walked over to where the relieving crew were waiting.

"Marty Smith," he said to the driver, who looked very pale but held out his hand in return.

"Jem Braithwaite, and my fireman is Harry Jones. I'm sorry to do this to you, but we've been on for ten hours already and I'm not feeling the best at all."

They all climbed into the cab of the big freight 8F; Marty looked around, noting his position was on the left, according to LMS practice. "You think you can manage the firing, Lance?"

"Yep, Mr Smith, I 'ad to fire an LMS tankie to Liverpool once an' 'ad no trouble. They even paid me a five-bob bonus!"

Marty laughed. "Yes, I heard about that; we also heard that you spent it the same day in Lime Street!"

Lance face turned red. "Very unkind that, Mr Smith. I suppose Mr Denton told you?"

"No, he didn't. I asked him and he said he knew nothing about it." In fact, Lance had met a Liverpool tart while on a break from a Birkenhead run and had boasted later among the cleaners in Chester shed of his conquest.

While they were talking, Harry Jones was checking the fire and the gauges to see whether their 8F was ready for the off. "Could you couple 'er up, Lance, while I put a few more shovelfuls around the box?"

Lance nodded and dropped down from the cab, glad to be away from the embarrassing turn of the conversation. On his return, Harry asked how long he had been on shift. Lance told him and he replied, "Then how about we fire half-hour turns each to Winchester an' I'll do the rest on the Southern? I've often fired an 8F and it's going to the shed there anyway."

"Yep, fine by me. Ta." Lance was pleased that he'd get a few breaks.

Jem sat on the driver's seat and watched for the signals while Marty handled the regulator and followed the other driver's signal observations. The four-man team performed very well, and with the signals largely in their favour they made good time to Newbury, where the senior official came along the platform to the cab again to enquire how they were managing.

"Very well, sir," replied Marty, leaning out of the cab. "We should be fine to Southampton."

"I'm relieved to hear it, Driver Smith. And er, by the way, you can forget any nonsense about insolence. My younger colleague has been chatting to the brigadier and has changed his mind!" He chuckled.

"Thank you, sir!"

The guard's whistle and green flag indicated a start, and they were immediately off again, Jem guiding Marty through the Newbury junction signals and on to the branch line towards Churn. It seemed to both Marty and Lance as they worked their way through the downs and over the Southern mainline to the west that their 8F was master of the heavy train.

With Lance and Harry changing over every half-hour, and with Driver Braithwaite advising Marty on the distinctive features of the line, the next stage of the run was straightforward for all four men. Even Jem Braithwaite seemed to recover slightly, although his face was still very pale.

As they were leaving Winchester, Harry said, "Right, Lance, you can put your shovel down now and relax; I'll take her from here."

"Ta very much 'arry." Lance sat on the fireman's seat. "Geez, I'm buggered!"

The rest of the run via Eastleigh was straightforward, but their arrival in Southampton Station was greeted with surprised amusement by a porter. "I'll never get used to this," he chuckled, "North-Eastern coaches, an LMS engine, from Great Western tracks now on the Southern. I wonder when we'll see Northern Ireland stock arriving!"

Marty, under the direction of Driver Jem Braithwaite, drew the train slowly through the main station and on to the docks where he entered a siding next to a hotel. Near this was a large shed into which the train's passengers disembarked. Other soldiers began unloading the two vans of the train and carrying large packing cases into the shed.

The brigadier passed them, growling to Marty, "Thanks to your railway company, Driver, we're very late!"

The senior railway official had come up in time to hear this. "You are quite mistaken, Brigadier. My information is that much of the lateness was occasioned by matters beyond our control: false information to the railways by yourself regarding incorrect train weight and van requirements, not to mention irritating and querulous complaints during the trip, wasting our time. A full report will go to your superiors with a recommendation that any future request from the army for railway assistance not be handled by you."

The brigadier turned away, his face red with anger but, saying nothing, he stamped away, fuming.

"That annoyed the bastard nicely!" Marty grinned at Lance and the other crew. "I don't mind admitting when I'm at fault, but I won't have another bugger's mistakes on my shoulders, not even pompous brigadier-generals'!"

15 - The War Ends
(June 1945)

The country was ecstatic. Germany had been soundly defeated, the Nazis overthrown, and peace in Europe had been signed. For many days, things were somewhat confused as people began to realise that they didn't have to worry about losing their menfolk, blackouts, air raid shelters, or bombing; even some rationing might be lifted. They began to think more positively about their futures.

At railway companies' headquarters, management officials began to search out post-war plans, which had been quietly considered with the bare outlines noted.

In the locomotive sheds at the rock-face, so to speak, senior foremen were totting up lists of repairs and sorting them according to urgency (most were listed as urgent). These included rolling-stock repairs, strengthening or replacing temporary repairs to trackwork, buildings, signalling equipment and the like. Eager young draftsmen in the various drawing offices were preparing plans for new locomotives or other vehicles which were badly needed. Other, pre-war, plans which had been abandoned were hauled out to be looked at again to see whether, in the new circumstances, they could offer useful suggestions.

In the running sheds, there was an air of cheer everywhere; the railwaymen could see an end to their very difficult shifts. It was sincerely hoped that fifteen- and twenty-hour shifts would be a thing of the past, and they could be expected home at the planned time more often.

In Reading shed one morning at the end of June, Driver Ivor Morris saw his mate Fireman Ben Goodwin coming towards him with a face like thunder.

"I know, Ben, what's troubling you," he greeted him cheerfully. "You lost a half crown and found a shilling!"

But Ben's expression didn't change. "No Ivor, that's not it. I found this pamphlet from the local Conservative Party promising that now that the war has ended, they want to build a 'Country Fit for Heroes'!" He handed the paper over to his driver.

"Ah," Ivor nodded seriously, studying it. "Yes, I see what you mean, Ben. You were only a sprog when the last lot finished, but I remember we were promised the same then."

"Exactly!"

"And all we got was the General Strike of '26 followed by the Great Depression of the early '30s, when half of us were out of work and hungry." Ivor shook the paper angrily. "How could the fools who put this out expect to win with rubbish like this? Do they think we're stupid or can't remember?"

"Now don't get me wrong, Ivor. I know Churchill's been the main reason for us not losing the war; I acknowledge that – who wouldn't? But when have his Conservatives ever done anything useful for the working classes? I want people in charge who will make sure I have a job, somewhere to live; decent schools and doctors I can afford!"

"I couldn't agree more, Ben." Ivor nodded emphatically as they both heard grunts of approval and clapping. They looked round in surprise to see other enginemen listening and expressing their agreement, with one annoyed exception.

Fireman Henry Grant walked up to Ben and poked him on the chest. "You want to kick Churchill out after everything he's done for us, Ben? Are you serious?"

"I am, Henry, make no mistake. Churchill's been a brilliant war leader; nobody could possibly doubt that, but is he the man to run a country at peace? No. I'll be voting for Atlee and the Labour Party!" Again, there were murmurs of acknowledgement from most of the listeners. Henry just shook his head angrily and stalked away.

"Fireman Goodwin! You aren't running a political meeting in company time, are you?" The call came from the shed foreman, who appeared among the group to hear the end of the discussion.

"Er, no sir!" Ben grinned and joined Ivor and others heading for the running shed. Everyone liked and respected the foreman, but no-one wanted to be in his bad books.

Ivor and Ben climbed on to their Prairie to begin its preparation for the day's shift. They were booked on local commuter work between Paddington and Reading all day; a relatively straightforward shift. After an hour or so their engine was ready, and they moved to the carriage sidings to collect their train of eight corridors and bring it to the platform where crowds of passengers were already gathering. There was a heavy and frequent service between the two stations with both fast and stopping trains, quite apart from the expresses from the west or South Wales, which were mostly non-stop. The commuter trains often had 2-6-2T Prairies in charge as these tank engines had a fine turn of speed when needed but could equally well handle trains which had to stop at every station in between.

On this fine early July morning, the waiting passengers gave a quite unusual impression which Ivor noticed as they drew in. A few were avidly studying their papers while most others were gossiping cheerfully. It was totally different to the usual silent or morose faces of the past six years that the two enginemen had got used to.

"Everyone's so chirpy today, Ben, it's lovely to see!"

"Yes Ivor, it's a new experience not to have to worry about doodlebugs or those blasted V2s exploding around you."

"Just think, Ben, we'll be buying our meat and two veg without having to dig out our ration books next!"

"Can't wait!" Ben put a couple of shovelfuls of coal down the right of the firebox where a hole was beginning to form. He was unaware that shopping without a ration book was to be still years away.

But not all passengers were happily ready for the day's work. As Ivor was slowing down to enter Slough, Ben called out urgently, "Passenger too close to the platform edge, Ivor!"

Ivor dropped the regulator and applied the emergency brakes to the train, which immediately began to shudder violently as it slowed down, but Ben could see it was too slow to stop in time for the man on the platform. He was swaying around, waving a bottle happily, far too close to the platform edge and totally oblivious to his danger. He swung his left arm out and although the locomotive's boiler front missed it, the front corner of the side tank smacked into his elbow, breaking it and smashing the bottle into shards of glass. A nearby passenger had rushed to seize him and held him from falling into the gap between the platform and the slowing train. He dragged the moaning man further back on the platform as horrified passengers hurried up to help.

When the train finally came to a grinding halt halfway along the platform, Ivor scurried over to the platform side of the cab.

"Did we hit him, Ben?" he enquired anxiously and stared out of the cab side.

"Yes, I'm afraid we did. But at least he didn't fall into the platform gap," replied Ben, gazing worriedly back. "Someone grabbed him and probably saved the stupid sod's life!"

"Look, Ben, you stay here and keep an eye on things, and I'll go and see how the man is." Ivor dropped to the platform and hurried along to where passengers were seeing to the injured man. A police constable was already there and the siren of an ambulance could be heard in a neighbouring street. Moments later, two ambulance ladies appeared with a stretcher and quickly laid the groaning man on it, covering him with a blanket, while the constable began questioning bystanders, noting down the details.

"How is the injured man, miss?" asked Ivor of the older of the two ladies.

She looked at him, noting his clothing. "Are you the train driver?"

Ivor nodded. "We couldn't stop in time. He was very lucky: I didn't even see him and my fireman happened to glance out of the cab just as we approached. Will he live?"

"He very likely will," she replied, "in spite of his foolishness, but I don't imagine he will ever use his left arm again. I'm not a doctor but that looks very bad, and I would expect it to be amputated." She stared at Ivor, "But please don't quote me on that; I'm not qualified to give a medical opinion."

"No," said Ivor, "of course not."

As he turned to leave, a furious passenger came up to him; this man seemed to be drunk as well.

"You the bloody train driver?" he demanded.

"I am. Why?" Ivor stared at the man.

"Why did you try to kill my mate, you bastard?"

Ivor paused to control himself before answering. "Why on earth would I try to kill him?" he asked, startled. "I don't even know him."

The man thought for a second, then snapped, "You could've stopped the train!"

"I did stop the train." Ivor pointed out.

"Not in damn time!"

"Tell me something," Ivor said curiously, "how would you stop a 200-ton train travelling at thirty miles an hour inside thirty yards?"

The man mumbled something but was grabbed by the throat: a very large workman had arrived, equally angry. "Come on, yer dopey drunken twat! Tell us before I belt yer one in the kisser!"

By this time the stationmaster, in company with a constable, arrived and the policeman pulled the workman back. "Nobody's beltin' anyone in the kisser on my patch!" he said vigorously. "That'd be a breach o' the peace, an' I'm not 'avin' it!"

"Get back into your cab, Driver," said the stationmaster to Ivor. "I'll see to this while you get the train away; we don't want to interrupt the timetable any more than necessary."

"Yessir," nodded Ivor and walked back gratefully to the cab as the passengers, now with nothing more to watch, boarded the train. The mood was suddenly more sombre.

Back in the cab, Ivor shook his head sadly. "Six years of war ended, Ben, and one stupid bloke gets drunk and loses his arm!"

"We had a teacher once who said he never punished stupid kids because they punished themselves so often," responded Ben.

"You had a wise teacher."

The day, which had started so promisingly, ended for them on a sad note.

***

Driver George Denton and Fireman Lance Hargreaves drew up at Hooton on their way with a stopper to Birkenhead. They had seen a cheerful group on the platform, some with party hats and carrying bottles of various types of alcohol: beer, spirits and wines, probably hoarded during the war. There was a charabanc in the yard, and the group was making its way towards it.

"Looks like some of 'em are 'avin' a party somewhere, Mr D," commented Lance with what sounded to George like envy in his voice.

"I bet you'd like to join them, Lance!" smiled George.

Lance had eyes for one young lady in the group. "I 'ave ter say I wouldn't mind 'avin' a drink with one of 'em."

George followed Lance's eyes. "The one you're looking at doesn't know how lucky she is," he teased. "You're too busy today to chat her up!"

"I think you mean unlucky, Mr D," laughed Lance. "When I was in 'ospital a couple of years back, the nurses all wanted ter chat ter me."

"Yes, and I wonder how many regretted it afterwards!"

"If they did, they never told me!"

George chuckled again. *Why don't I ever get the last word?*

Once more George remembered how lucky they had been on that day; they had been close to where a doodlebug had exploded, and both had ended up in hospital. Lance had almost lost his leg.

"What are you going to do in your next week's leave, Lance?" he asked, changing the subject.

"I'm goin' ter get meself fit, Mr D. I'm goin' campin' next week. I bought meself a sleepin' bag, special."

"Next week?"

"Yep. Walkin' in Delamere Forest; Monday ter Wednesday with Mary 'iggins, an' Thursday ter Saturday with Sandra 'awks! We're celebratin' the war's end."

"And do either of these young ladies know about the other?" enquired George with interest.

"Getaway, Mr D, o' course not! They wouldn't be 'appy if they knew, an' if they wasn't 'appy, they wouldn't enjoy themselves walkin' with me, would they!"

George couldn't help himself; he laughed out loud at Lance's logic.

The following week George was on miscellaneous duties 'As Required' until his fireman returned from leave, and he was regaling the story to driver Dick Osbourne in the enginemen's mess over a mug of tea in the late evening.

"Let's see now," said Dick, thinking. "Today's Tuesday evening, so what's the betting he has Miss Higgins in his sleeping bag by now?"

"No takers," grinned George.

Dick pulled his watch from his waistcoat and glanced at it. "Hmm, ten fifty-seven," he said and picked up his mug and turned to go. "Must be off, George, we're preparing a Hall for the 12.10 to Salop, and I need to keep an eye on young Cardew; he's got the makings of a good fireman."

The rest of the week's shifts for George varied from shunting in Chester and Saltney, two days on commuter trains to Birkenhead, and a day's shift to replace an ill driver on the Paddington express to Wolverhampton and return. But his thoughts kept drifting to the antics of his fireman, recalling his own lecherous days on leave in Paris during the first War; he too had been active, although later, back in the UK, he had been too busy with his job until he met his Alice. After that no other woman had interested him.

"How was your camping week, Lance?" he asked his mate on Lance's return to duty.

"Mixed, Mr D, mixed," replied Lance, shovelling busily without making any further comment.

George nodded; he knew that meant that something had gone wrong. "Sorry to hear that."

"Yeah, Sandra found out about Mary an' changed 'er mind about campin' with me."

"Did you enjoy Delamere Forest at all?"

Lance perked up. "Yeah, we stayed an extra day in the sunny weather!"

"How was the walking?"

"Walkin'? What walkin'?" asked Lance.

"Didn't you tell me you were going walking in the forest?"

"Oh yeah, I might've done. Nah, we didn't; she said 'er feet hurt."

'Well, what else—" George began, then stopped and said, "Never mind." There was no need to ask what else they had been engaged in; George felt he already knew.

They were manning a Mogul on a passenger to Manchester; the LMS Jubilee had failed, and the LMS had requested assistance from the GWR Chester shed for a replacement engine, which had been granted. The railway companies had realised that the government control during the war had encouraged a closer co-operation between them, which had improved services.

Lance gazed out of the cab several times after they left Warrington; he had not been on the Manchester run for two or three years and wanted to see what changes had been made. He noted the vast Vulcan engineering complex near Earlestown and stared in awe at the locomotive on the siding outside it.

"Cor, Mr D, didja see that huge Pacific we just passed? It was bigger than one of our Kings and on'y on narrer gauge!"

"Probably for South Africa, Lance."

The Manchester approaches showed that the city, like Liverpool and Birkenhead, had received plenty of attention from the Luftwaffe. *Poor Buggers!* thought Lance as they pulled into Manchester Exchange. *Thank God it's all over!*

***

Gradually, the jubilation at the cessation of hostilities in September – when the Japanese finally surrendered – came to an end, and life began to take back its normal routine in Britain. Trains were still full, albeit many with returned servicemen, while locomotives and rolling stock were badly need of proper repairs. The difficulty the railway companies continued to face was that the new Labour government saw little reason to assist them financially more than previously agreed when it had already decided to nationalise them. Consequently, they continued to struggle with repairs and maintenance, and the travelling public returned to its predictable grumbling about poor service.

Driver Trevor Bentley and his fireman Joe Lennox were sitting in the cab of their Prairie in Birmingham's Moor Street Station; they had half an hour to wait before they could return to Stratford-on-Avon.

Trevor was smoking a cigarette when a workman sitting on a nearby bench got up and strolled over to them.

"You railway fellahs nothin' better ter do?" he asked truculently.

Trevor sat up and leaned down towards the man. "What would you suggest?"

"Get off yer arses and do somethin' useful. Yer trains're still bloody late, an' 'alf ov 'em aren't fit ter be seen."

"We had a few problems during the war," countered Trevor mildly.

"Yeah, but the war's over; yer could 'ave new trains by now!"

"Did you have problems during the war?" inquired Trevor.

"Course we did; we was bombed out! I 'ave ter live wiv me bloody in-laws."

Trevor smiled at the man. "As you said, the war's over now, so why haven't you got a new house?"

With an angry grunt, the man stamped off in a huff.

Joe cackled. "He had no answer to that, Trev, did he?"

"No, Joe, and of course we do have better stock." Trevor patted the backhead of their Prairie. "A year ago, we had constant trouble with this and had to make do, as it were. Now they've finally been able to get it into the works and fix it properly."

"Yeah," Joe said, "it's definitely running more smoothly, and it's not the only one. I was talking to Driver Hepworth from Worcester last week and he was saying that one of their Halls had been to the works after months of requests from his shed. Now it's a pleasure to drive, he told me."

"The recovery will be slow, Joe, but it'll get done now we don't have air raids and bombs to contend with, but anyone expecting miracles is going to be disappointed!"

16 - 'I Don't Feel No Different!' (Dec 1947)

It was five o'clock in the morning, pitch-dark and very cold, on a late December day when George Denton looked at the duty roster. He noted the details and then walked to the enginemen's mess to find his fireman.

"First a short run, Lance: 6.26 passenger to Woodside," George began, "then we pick up an Acton fitted freight as far as 'hampton, light engine from there to Wellington, where we exchange with an Oxford crew and return on a parcels to Chester."

Lance nodded; he had already seen their roster for the day and had already checked the fire of their 51xx Prairie tank engine, cleaned the cab and was ready for their first mug of tea.

"Righto, George, an' I've built up the fire as well as me thirst. An' I'm glad we've a tankie to kick off with today, it's a bleedin' cold mornin'." Prairie tank engines had enclosed cabs and were welcome places in cold weather.

They had time for a mug of tea before they could move their engine over to the station's Platform Three, ready to take their train to Birkenhead Woodside. The train was a local stopper which brought daily workers from Chester and the Wirral to the docks at Birkenhead and Liverpoool. Promptly on time, the points for the Birkenhead direction clicked over and the starter signal dropped to the clear. George glanced back out of the cab to see the guard raise his green flag and they were cleared to move off. He nudged the regulator carefully upwards and the engine began to ease the train out of the platform, across the switches and past the GWR shed on the right. By the time they reached the Hoole Road bridge they were steaming well. They paused briefly at the little halt at Upton-by-Chester to pick up a few more dock workers and continued to the other stations to Birkenhead Woodside, collecting more workers each time.

As they reached Birkenhead, Lance commented, "It's nice ter 'ave an engine in good nick again, George."

During the war years, enginemen had to put up with locomotives well past their repair dates because the workshops were busy not only maintaining engines but they had also been required to provide war materials. Many workshops were well known to have pools of very skilled metal- and wood-workers who could adapt to building weapons; Swindon had built fifty midget submarines and parts for bombers. But now, over two years after the war's end, George and Lance's Prairie had returned from Wolverhampton works after a refurbishment and it had been newly painted. They had an hour's wait before their next duty and time for a comfortable mug of tea and a sticky bun before they had to return to Chester.

"Any special plans for Christmas, Lance?" asked George. "No - wait. I bet you've got some unsuspecting girl lined up?"

"No, George. I did 'ave one: a blonde with great ti— but no matter. 'Er parents moved ter Manchester sudden, like. I dunno why."

"Perhaps her parents heard that she'd met you?" replied George with a grin.

"Unkind, George, unkind!"

They both laughed.

George pulled a coin from his pocket. "This shilling says you'll have another girl lined up within a week!"

"Funny you should say that. There's this Brenda, 'oo tole me last week, if I ever wanted ter—"

George laughed again and handed the shilling to Lance. "One of these days, Lance my lad, you're going to meet one who will make you do what she wants!"

"I'm 'opin' that's this Brenda!"

George shook his head, picked up his mug, and drank deeply. *You just can't win with this lad!* he thought. *I'll just keep my mouth shut! My pocket too*, he added to himself.

Their next duty was for a fitted freight as far as Oxley sidings in Wolverhampton, returning to Chester on a Birkenhead express. But a surprise awaited them: a very powerful 47XX express freight class 2-8-0 at Birkenhead shed; it had recently been in Wolverhampton Works and had been thoroughly repaired. These huge engines were sometimes even used on express passenger duties if a Castle or a County were not available.

"That's odd," remarked George as he saw it, "this 47 had a major repair and has been cleaned but not repainted." It was normal for locomotives undergoing a major repair to be given a new coat of paint these days.

"Shortage o' paint somewhere?" commented Lance without great interest; he was looking forward to firing a newly serviced firebox.

George was still wondering at the failure to repaint the engine while he began to move the locomotive. He took the engine over to the sidings where their freight waited, backed slowly to the vans, and stopped so that Lance could drop down and lift the coupling hook onto the front van and screw in the vacuum brake pipe.

With vacuum brakes, there was better control over the whole train; an unfitted or loose freight needed much more careful handling. Even so, after receiving the clear signal from the yard, George moved out slowly onto the main line and began to accelerate southwards.

It was immediately obvious that the repairs to the locomotive had been effective. She moved easily and smoothly with the van train and George and Lance looked forward to an enjoyable trip. However, they were to be disappointed.

At Saltney yard they were signalled back to pick up five more vans, which took another fifteen minutes, then in Wrexham a signal held them on the main line for the loss of ten more while a careless signalman had allowed another movement across the main lines in front of them.

"Daft sod should a' let us through first," complained Lance.

"He may not have had a choice," explained George. "The engine moving across may have been slower than expected."

"Well, 'e should a' thought o' that before 'e let 'em across," said Lance, aggrieved.

"Your new Brenda wouldn't like hearing you complaining, I'm sure!" laughed George.

Lance cheered up at the thought of that evening's entertainment with his new girl. "I'm 'opin' she won't 'ave to!"

But their bad luck continued. At Coleham yard in Shrewsbury, they pulled in once more to detach two vans and add four more: the shunt causing the loss of another twenty-five minutes. Fortunately, they were not held up again and passed through Wellington at almost express passenger speed, arriving in Oxley Sidings only thirty-seven minutes late. While their train was remarshalled, they took the locomotive to fill up with water, Lance cleaned the cab, and they took it to back onto the train again, ready for the new crew. Once they had chatted to the new men, they walked back to the Stafford Road shed to join their engine waiting to take over the Paddington to Birkenhead express from the King which had brought the train from Paddington. Their replacement engine as far as Chester was a new County class 4-6-0.

"We get a nice, repaired engine ter run a fast freight an' wot 'appens? We can't give 'er a chance ter belt along. We get stopped every five bloody minutes! Then we 'ave a new County an' I bet we get stopped at signals every now and agen!"

"Come on, Lance; you've been in cabs for over ten years now. Haven't you got used to that yet?" George remonstrated. "Try and think of a couple of runs we might have today: think of the stretch north of Salop and then the run from Wrexham down Gresford Bank!"

"Yeah, George, I s'pose you're right. They might be easy if this 'ere County's in good nick."

As Lance spoke, the servicing fireman descended from the cab of their County 4-6-0 and heard his comment.

"Afternoon, George and young Lance," he greeted them. "You don't have to worry. 1016's running nicely; my mate and I took her to Oxford two days back, and she's fine!"

"That's good news, Bill," replied George. "Hear that, Lance? Nothing to worry about!"

They backed their County out of the shed yard and into the station, where they were left on the down main through line so that when the Birkenhead came in the train engine and coaches to be detached could move off, then they could back on. Right on time, the Birkenhead express appeared in the distance, slowing down for the stop.

"There," said George, "she's on time after a long run. With luck, we can keep time for the rest of the run to Chester and after that it's someone else's job!"

The train engine was a mighty King and, as soon as a porter had uncoupled the first four coaches, it moved slowly off with them to the coach sidings where they would be cleaned and serviced before the next day's return. The King would then go to the shed for a similar service.

The prediction of the Wolverhampton fireman came true: their County was only two years old and had been run in nicely. Many drivers did not like these new engines, but George took to them quickly and he showed Lance how to get the best out of them. The run down Gresford Bank was a treat; they were able to make up time that a longer stop in Ruabon had cost them when an elderly passenger had been taken ill, and a doctor had had to be called. They arrived in Chester two minutes ahead of time.

"Got a little Christmas present for your new girl, Lance?" queried George with a smile as they walked to the shed to book off duty.

"Yep, it's in me pocket," replied Lance as they unlocked their lockers to pull out their overcoats.

"Have you a venue planned for tonight?" asked George.

"A venue? Wot's that?"

"It's where you plan to meet and entertain yourselves," replied George, wishing he hadn't asked; he realised he would rather not know.

"Yeah, we're meetin' outside the town 'all."

"Well, I'll see you on Boxing Day then, Lance. Have a nice Christmas."

"Yeah, ta, George; and the same to you and Mrs Denton." With that, Lance pulled a scarf out of his pocket and a small packet dropped out onto the floor.

"Oops," muttered Lance, "Brenda's Christmas present."

George sighed as he saw it: a packet of condoms. *I should have guessed.*

A few days later, George and Lance took another Prairie on a stopping passenger to Wellington as far as Ruabon, where they exchanged with a Salop crew to take the train further south. In Ruabon they boarded a Barmouth stopper on the cushions, travelling in comfort as far as Corwen, where they were scheduled to pick up a local goods just before midnight to take it to Birkenhead. As they left Corwen en route to Birkenhead and trundled slowly back east through Llangollen, they passed a down passenger waiting in the station. The driver of the Mogul in charge gave a long whistle. Lance glanced over in surprise to see who was greeting them, but he didn't recognise either man. As they left the station, the little Prairie tank engine waiting in the up refuge platform siding also whistled.

"Did you see the crew on that Mogul, George?" Lance asked.

George shook his head. "No, who were they?"

"Dunno, but they whistled at us."

"At us? Why?"

Lance frowned, sending his mind back, then said, "Er p'raps they were whistlin' at the crew of the Prairie; it might not 'ave been us at all."

George nodded; he was more concerned with listening to the motion of the engine; one of the coupling rods sounded loose. He brought their train to a gentle stop just outside the station.

"Lance, slip out and tell the signalman that I am going to have a look at the engine's motion."

"Righto." Lance put his shovel down and peeped into the firebox. The fire was burning quite well and could be left for five minutes before it would need more attention. He climbed down to the track and made his way the hundred yards back to the signal cabin.

The window in the cab opened and a head peered out at him. "Trouble, Lance?" asked the bobby.

"Yeah," replied Lance. "Mr Denton's not 'appy with the motion. He's goin' ter 'ave a quick shufti."

Lance turned round and walked back to the engine. George was down on the side, using a hammer to tap the coupling rod where it was attached to the driving wheel. He muttered something Lance didn't catch and climbed back into the cab.

"It'll get us to Chester, Lance, but we'll need a fitter there to tighten it up. Slip out again and give the signal man the details and tell him to ring Chester for a fitter to be ready to check the locomotive when we get there."

Lance nodded and walked back to the signal cabin with the message.

"Aye, I'll phone 'em now," responded the bobby and he disappeared rapidly back into the warmth of the cabin.

When Lance arrived back in the cab, George was already standing with the regulator in his hand, ready to get their train moving once more. "All done?"

"Yep, 'e said 'e'd ring Chester straightaway."

"Fine," said George and lifted the regulator. Their train moved slowly off again. Lance checked the fire to see that all was well. The gauge showed enough steam pressure for only a couple of shovelfuls of coal to bring it up to a satisfactory level. From then the run was no problem through the Dee Valley and through Ruabon and Wrexham, but after running down Gresford Bank even Lance could hear the clanking noise emanating from the driver's side.

George frowned but said nothing as the engine laboured up through Saltney Junction and onto the LMS main North Wales line to Chester. They were signalled into a siding near the Chester GWR shed and a fitter came out with a bag of tools and waited while they came to a stop, then he climbed into the cab.

"What's the problem, George?"

George explained and they both went down to examine the offending rod. The fitter tapped it and nodded. "Yep, it's loose; I can tighten it now and you can be on your way again in twenty minutes; it'll get you to Birkenhead, but it'll need proper attention there." Then he looked at it again. "Ah, an Aberdare; I doubt it will get any more attention except from a Birkenhead fitter who will remove the rods for a pilot engine to lead it to the scrap siding! Get yourselves a mug of tea; I won't be too long."

"It's teatime, Lance," chuckled George, back in the cab. "Fred is giving us twenty minutes. Then we can be off again to Birkenhead, and you can be off meeting some unfortunate maiden again this evening."

"Can't do that tonight, George," grinned Lance. "I'm meetin' a new bird tonight an' she don't yet know how lucky she'll be!"

George shook his head. "One of these days, Lance, my lad, you're going to chat up another girl with a big husband, and he'll want to use you as a punch bag, like that one four years back!"

"Don't remind me!" Lance suddered. He had chatted up a pretty girl on the way to Shrewsbury and arranged to see her again on her return the following day, but her large, very angry, boyfriend had come to see Lance instead. George had hidden Lance behind the boiler and misdirected the boyfriend, thus saving the fireman's bacon.

But Lance's mind was on a different plane; he had just seen a Castle with a Birkenhead express entering the General Station.

What the 'ell was that written on the tender? An' the linin' looks funny! He shook his head. *Shouldn't 'ave 'ad that extra whisky las' night.*

"Something up, Lance? You look puzzled."

"Did yer see that Castle wot just came in with the Birken'ead?"

"No, why?"

"It looked a bit diff'rent, that's all."

"Different how?"

"Dunno really, jus' diff'r'nt."

"It was probably newly painted – that would look different!"

Then George realised. A major change had occurred on the railways: they had been nationalised overnight. It was now 1948 and they were all now 'British Railways'. That was what Lance had seen on the tender! The GWR had become the Western Region of British Railways.

He turned to Lance. "Do you realise, Lance, that you are now a different class of citizen?"

Lance stopped shovelling and looked at his driver in surprise. "Wot?"

"You're no longer a simple Great Western Fireman."

"I'm not?" Lance shook his head. His driver did not usually talk nonsense.

"By no means," said George.

"Wot am I then?" demanded Lance indignantly.

"As from today you're a Civil Servant."

"A Civil Servant?" Lance was nonplussed.

"Well, 'civil' might not be entirely appropriate in your case, of course." George corrected himself. "Perhaps 'government employee' might be a more accurate description."

Lance glared at his driver. "Wot the 'ell are yer talking about, George?"

"Don't you read the newspapers, Lance? Apart, of course, from looking to see if Jane strips off again?" (Jane was a pretty girl in a popular comic strip at the time.)

"Course I do."

"But you didn't know that the Great Western Railway – the company you have been working in for fifteen years – no longer exists?"

"It doesn't?" Lance glanced unbelievingly at the Paddington express with its cream and brown coaches, standing ready for departure across on Platform Two.

"It does not."

"Well, 'oo the fu—" He stopped abruptly. "'Oo're we workin' for then?"

"The government, Lance. We have been nationalised!"

"We've bin wot?"

"Nationalised."

"When did this 'appen?"

"Last night at midnight." George was enjoying himself; it wasn't often he had his young mate at a loss.

"Midnight?"

"Yes; remember all that whistling as we passed through Llangollen?"

"Yeah."

"That was the end of the GWR. We are now servants of British Railways, Western Region!"

"That right?" Lance bent to shovel coal into the firebox. "Well, I don't feel no different!"

17 - Do Britannias Rule the Rails? (May 1953)

"What the hell's this coming in?" Driver Norman Benson stared at the incoming locomotive arriving at Shrewsbury's Coleham WR shed. As it curved in, he could see it was a Pacific with large windshields and what appeared to be an LMS boiler front, but with a very high running plate it clearly wasn't a Duchess. In any case, it was entering the Western shed. Any visiting LMR Duchess would be serviced at the London Midland Region shed next door.

"That, dear boy, is one of the new Britannias," remarked Driver Jeremy Murgatroyd. "They're said to be able to match our Castles, but I cannot guarantee that as I have yet to drive one."

The Britannias were 4-6-2 Pacifics designed by British Railways as mixed traffic engines which could cover a wide range of duties over many of the nation's routes. They were planned for ease of maintenance and with improvements gleaned from a study in 1948 of major locomotive types from the previous private companies.

The locomotive pulled up and Driver Paul Todmorden climbed down to growl at the two enginemen waiting to service it.

"'Eap o' shit!" he snapped. "Its levers 're all over the bloody place, and you've got to drive on the left-'and side. It's worse for my mate: 'e 'as to fire on the right an' 'e's right-'anded!"

Paul's fireman, Jeff Hodges, nodded his agreement as he strode away.

"What's more," added Paul, "we've just come up from Bristol an' it can't do anythin' a Castle can't do. If we need new engines, why can't the buggers at the Kremlin in Marylebone ask Swindon to build more Castles? We already know 'ow to do it; no need to spend all that money designin' a new engine we don't bloody need!"

"Perhaps it needs more running in and checking for minor improvements, Paul," Murgy pointed out reasonably. "Look at what happened to our Manors."

The Manors were originally built in 1938 to replace elderly Moguls and initially disappointed drivers because the war began before they could be properly assessed; after the war, they were thoroughly checked, and with only minor alterations they proved to be excellent engines for lighter routes.

"That's as may be, Murgy, but we should be spendin' our money on lookin' at our flamin' Counties, too. They're nearly as strong as Castles an' cheaper, but they won't climb 'ills."

"Ah, now Paul, have you ever spoken to a Chester driver, one George Denton Esquire? He knows how to get the best out of the Counties; he likes them."

"'E's welcome to 'em!" grunted Paul, walking back to book off duty.

"Not sufficient patience, our Paul," remarked Murgy to nobody in particular as he walked back into the mess. Here he met with Jeff Hodges, and repeated the observation.

"You're right of course, Murgy," replied Jeff. "He's not happy with anything new. You should hear him about the new colour schemes. He claims the mixed traffic Counties, Halls and Granges have become LNWR engines with their black paint and red-and-white lining, and what he says about the coaches in their blood and custard is enough to embarrass any passing vicar!"

Murgy laughed. "I have not heard him on that particular topic, but I must concur with you on that: his language is impressive in both its vulgarity and ingenuity!"

There was some laughter in the mess; Murgy was a popular man whose contributions to the general conversation were listened to eagerly. They were often witty, very rarely negative, and generally highly entertaining. There was common agreement too, that on railway matters Driver Jeremy Murgatroyd, despite his amusing presence, was nobody's fool.

"However," the man continued, "I have wondered on occasion whether the men who crew these Britannias are prone to falling out of their cabs. Their locomotives have a cab door which we Western men seem to have generally managed without for – er, let me see now – the last one hundred years."

There was a loud burst of laughter at this; most of them had at one time or another teased BR drivers about falling out of their cabs. Yet there was little doubt that the range of Riddles' new BR designs paid more attention to the comfort of enginemen than the old GWR ever had.

Driver Benson smiled mischievously as he asked loudly, "Murgy, what's your duty today, do you know yet?"

"Um, no, Sandy. I haven't yet checked the board."

"Did I just hear you say you hadn't driven a Britannia yet?"

"That is correct: you did. May I ask why?"

"I've just been to the board; you are to relieve Chester men here on the up Paddington. They failed their Castle, and you and Bill are to take a relieving engine on to Stafford Road and come back on the cushions; then you're on a Cardiff goods."

"That all sounds perfectly normal, so why are you smiling?"

"Your relieving engine is that Britannia that's just come in; it's needed at Stafford Road."

The listening men all guffawed; it wasn't often that Murgy got caught by surprise. He recovered himself quickly. "Well, 'that is the way' – as Americans tend to remark – 'the cookie crumbles'. Incidentally, what, pray, is a cookie?" He looked enquiringly around the group.

"It's a biskit, Murgy! Come down off yer 'igh 'orse!" Paul Todmorden cackled: he had quietly re-entered the mess. His fireman Jeff chuckled, pleased to see his driver in a good temper for a change.

"Thank you, Driver Todmorden, for your considerate advice which I shall gratefully accept."

Murgy smiled at Paul, who nodded and muttered to Jeff.

"I fink 'e's got a bloody dictionary inside 'is gob!"

Jeremy Arthur Murgatroyd was a major disappointment to his wealthy family. He had been sent to Eton and was booked into an Oxford college and was expected to enter the army following the long-standing family tradition. Yet during his Eton days he had discovered a deep fascination for the Great Western Railway and spent much of his spare time at nearby Windsor, observing the trains. In 1932 he had horrified his family by leaving school early and joining the GWR as a cleaner, but he had rapidly moved up the ladder and was now a senior driver.

"I shall endeavour to discover the veracity of Driver Benson's remarks in that part of my duty between here and Wolverhampton and subsequently report my own observations to you worthy gentlemen," he announced to the grinning men and left, adding, "Come along, Harold."

Fireman Harold Junkin followed on and the two men climbed into the cab of the Britannia, looking around with interest. Both were experienced in their duties and found that, although the cab layout was not what they were used to, they were quickly able to manage the new locomotive. They backed it out of the shed and along the short stretch into the station where they coupled up to the Paddington express, in place of the failed Castle.

The guard's green flag waved as his whistle sounded, and Murgy eased the regulator upwards. The engine took hold of its train without hesitation and began to move round to the left, past the triangle which contained one of the longest signal-boxes in the country, accelerating along the straight stretch on its way towards the next stop at Wellington. The three-quarter-hour run to Wolverhampton including the steep gradient out of Wellington Station proved no problem for the Britannia and when they stopped at Wolverhampton to uncouple and back into Stafford Road shed, Murgy looked at his fireman. "Now then, Harold, what do you think about this new engine?"

Fireman Junkin thought for a moment. "That short run is not enough of a test, Murgy, but I would say the Brit appears to be much on a par with our Castles, but whether it can run as well is still an open question."

"Thank you, that is exactly what I think. However, I will happily admit the cab is more comfortable!"

"Yes, that may be true, Murgy, but we firemen–" replied Harold with a wide grin on his face – "don't get much chance to sit down like an elderly driver with a sore arse!"

"Really, Harold, there is no call to be coarse!" Murgy spoke in mock offence. "Just wait until you're an aged driver with a sensitive rear end!"

Some weeks later, Jeremy found himself on an unusual duty: he and Harold were to relieve a Chester crew on a Paddington train and return to Wolverhampton and from there were on a fitted goods to Coleham yard.

"Where are we to relieve the Chester crew, sir?" the driver asked the shedmaster.

"Here at Salop, Murgy. You take their County to Stafford Road and from there you take that Britannia to Paddington. Paddington claims that it's been too long in the Wolverhampton Division and they want it back."

"Ah! We've been playing with it, sir, have we?"

"Something like that. Now, since you don't have to prepare the County, you and Junkin can have a free hour tomorrow while you wait for it to come in."

"You are all heart, sir."

Next morning, the Paddington express arrived on time in Shrewsbury and Murgy and Harold were waiting at the end of the platform where the County came to a stop and the two Salop men climbed into the cab.

"Any issues with this engine, Marty?" asked Driver Murgatroyd.

"No, Murgy, she's in good nick, but I've heard that you Salop men don't like the Counties." Marty Smith smiled. "Our George Denton has shown us how to get the best out of them."

"Yes, some of us are indeed sceptical. However, I have not driven them sufficiently often to form an opinion."

"Well now's your chance to get some more experience. Good luck." And with that, Marty Smith and his fireman left the cab.

On the run to the changeover at Wolverhampton, Murgy handled the County with care and attention, trying to think about what he had been told about these engines. When they pulled in at Wolverhampton, he had decided that he liked these engines and determined to have a word with George Denton next time they met. They left the cab as a servicing crew climbed in to take the County to the shed. The waiting Britannia backed on to their train and they climbed up to the cab, exchanging greetings with the descending crew.

"Now, Harold, let us see what we can do with this engine," remarked Murgy as he glanced over the controls and settled himself down on the comfortable seat on the left of the cab.

"I might be a bit slow today, Murgy," answered Harold. "Me being right-handed like and firing now on the right; it'll take some getting used to!"

"I expect you will manage, Harold, you usually do."

The train was of moderate weight with fourteen corridors; a normal Castle requirement. Kings would normally be used if the train exceeded fifteen or sixteen coaches. The Britannia seemed to cope quite well as far as Birmingham's Snow Hill station and handled the gradients with no trouble.

"What is that curious expression: 'so far, so good', Harold?"

"That sums it up."

"The next two hours should give us a clearer opinion."

"Yup." Harold was a man of few words; he was still trying to find an easy method of firing and, glancing at the cosy fireman's seat, wondered whether he would ever get to used it. Western engines had a short wooden board for their crews.

The two hours to Paddington showed that the Britannia was no worse than a Castle but racing through Bicester it showed a distinct tendency for roughness, so much so that a passenger alighting in Paddington stopped at the cab to enquire from Murgy whether he had had the hiccups during the run.

Harold turned quickly away to hide his amusement, quietly shaking with laughter. He turned back to Murgy. "I thought it was the Brit, Murgy, but was it your hiccups after all?"

Murgy look at him with disdain. "Your mockery, Harold, does you no credit," he said before he began to smile. "Hiccups!" he laughed. "Now I believe I have heard everything!"

At Old Oak Common shed when they pulled in to book off duty, another driver came over and introduced himself as Trevor Sanders.

"You just off the Birkenhead?" he asked Murgy.

"That is so," replied Jeremy, holding out his hand. "Jeremy Murgatroyd – generally known as 'Murgy' – from Salop shed at your service, sir."

"Been on the Western long, Murgy, have you?"

"Twenty years, Trevor, why do you ask?"

"I see you've come in with a Britannia. How does it compare with a Castle?"

Murgy paused, thinking. "About the same, I would judge.

Rather rough at speed through Bicester, however. What is your opinion?"

Trevor's teeth gleamed. "Magnificent! I've just transferred to the Western from Stratford in East London, and I can tell you, we've never had anything like them. The crews there reckon they're the bees' knees. We've been able to speed up our timetables for East Anglian expresses."

"I am glad to hear it, Trevor, however, we in the Western have had our Stars and Castles for forty years; we're used to good engines!" Murgy added with mischief in his eye, "And we don't much like the Britannias!"

A loud Welsh voice echoed from behind him as he spoke. "It's wrong you are there, Murgy!"

Murgy swung round in surprise and then pleasure. "Taff! I have not set eyes on you for many years. How are you?"

"Almost ready to retire, I am. I am now at Cardiff Canton and let me inform you that we Welshmen there think most Western drivers don't like the Brits only because they're left-hand drive!"

Taff's fireman added, "And they're too lazy to learn to change!"

Harold, greatly amused at all this, hurried away quickly. *It's not often that other enginemen get the better of Murgy*, he reflected. *Perhaps I should stay and enjoy it!*

But his driver and Taff were deep in friendly conversation catching up with each other, so he left them to it.

***

Driver Huw Gruffydd of Cardiff's Canton shed grumbled his disappointment to his fireman, Andy Philipps. "This bloody Castle's no good! She's only got twelve on and we're already fifteen minutes down, and haven't even reached the tunnel yet!"

The Severn Tunnel could be a problem for trains; although the downward gradient allowed some speed, the steep uphill climb slowed many. Additionally, the line was very busy, and sometimes heavy goods trains were excessively slow, forcing faster trains to wait. They were to take an ECS through to Paddington, changing engines at Swindon on the way.

"Yes, Huw, but we're Empty Stock, and there's no real weight to haul," Fireman Philipps countered. "And Swindon's getting this Castle to repair. We might get a freshly run-in engine for the rest of the run to Paddington."

"I hope you're right, Andy. I'm tired of this crawling with a so-called express passenger locomotive!"

"I don't know why you're complaining; we've often had an engine ready for a 'sole and heel', it's part of the job. At least we're taking it in to be seen to."

Driver Gruffydd just grunted. He liked his job, especially when he had a fast train. More than once he had been reprimanded for arriving well before time. There was an agreed speed for most stretches of track, which enginemen were supposed to keep to if possible; excessive speed could be dangerous if the track was not kept in good repair.

Andy Philipps sighed quietly. He knew Huw Gruffydd would speed again as soon as he could, tearing great holes in Andy's fire and forcing him to use more coal than was warranted. He made a quiet bet with himself that Huw would make up at least twelve of the fifteen minutes they had lost before they reached Swindon and changed engines.

When they drew up in Swindon, they were indeed on time.

Driver Gruffydd's eyes gleamed as he caught sight of the newly painted Britannia waiting on the nearby siding. This would surely be their engine for the Paddington run, fresh from the works! He rubbed his hands. "There you go, Andy," he said, pointing to the Britannia. "We're in for some fun at last!"

The fireman rolled his eyes and climbed down to uncouple their Castle as the Britannia moved forward to back on as soon as the Castle was clear. The servicing crew climbed up into their cab and exchanged details of the locomotives, and Huw and Andy left the Castle and walked to the Britannia, climbing up to the cab. Here everything was spotless and shining.

"A real engine!" gloated Huw. "Pity we've got no passengers to impress."

His fireman said nothing; with twelve empty coaches, a locomotive fresh out of the works and a broadly downhill run for two hours, there would be no holding his driver back! He prayed that signalmen would often hold them; if Huw was too fast, he might catch up with trains ahead and have to slow down. Andy sighed and checked his fire.

They were very soon racing through Shrivenham, riding roughly over the points and jerking the fireirons in their box on the tender. Andy glanced over to see whether Huw had noticed the roughness, but if he had, it was ignored.

"I hope to God that crossover in Challow has been fixed, Huw," shouted Andy across the noisy cab.

"You worry too much, Andy." Huw held the regulator firmly high as they tore through Uffington. Fortunately, the distant signal at Challow slowed them down and they could only crawl over the crossover before picking up speed again. Andy breathed a sigh of relief; had they raced through, that crossover was bad. Had they sped over it, they could very easily have derailed. Hopefully, heavy traffic at Didcot or Reading might slow us again but even then Huw could still manage a ton through Hanwell!

But Huw didn't wait until Hanwell.

They came off the road just before Steventon; at 57 mph, the front bogie of the Britannia hit a check rail and rode up over it, derailing the driving wheels while the locomotive, miraculously, stayed upright. The first three coaches shook under the sudden stop and derailed, forming a Z shape behind them on the track, one of them falling over on its side.

"Huw, you bloody idiot! If we'd had passengers, you'd have killed a dozen, us included!"

Clearly, this Britannia did not rule the rails.

18 - A Taunton Trauma
(July 1960)

One Saturday in early summer, the weather was glorious but the crew of the down Penzance express couldn't enjoy it as much as they had hoped because there was talk of replacing the Kings on the Riviera service. Their King was in top condition, having been to Swindon for its regular minor repair, yet in spite of this they had been held up both in Reading and in Westbury. Traffic had been heavy and they were running very late but hoping to make up some of the time before they reached Plymouth. The Taunton approach signals appeared and Herbie Campbell, the fireman of the Cornish Riviera Express, stared in astonishment.

"Bill!" he called to his driver, "the bloody Taunton signals are against us!"

"What? Bugger it! What are the bobbies doing to us? We're already an hour behind!" Driver William Clifford was furious; he detested being late at any time but with the Riviera it was almost a crime in his eyes, especially if his driving was responsible. Not that this was likely; Bill was one of Laira's best drivers, acknowledged both in Laira and Old Oak Common. However, this time there could be no argument: both the distant and the home signals were at danger. He slowed the train down and came to a stop, fortuitously next to the signal box.

"Hop out, Herbie, and find out what the sodding problem is. It must be quite serious for the bobby to have to stop us!"

Fireman Campbell nodded, climbed down to the track, and hurried up the steps to the box.

"What the hell's up here?" he demanded of the bobby.

The bobby grinned at him. "The King of the Road, no less? Well, mate, your King is up against a Warship!"

Herbie's eyebrows shot up. "What are you effing talking about?"

The bobby's face kept its grin. "There's a Warship ahead on your heavy relief train in Taunton and it's just been failed. They're waiting on a replacement engine and Taunton's only got a Mogul spare and they need another engine to double-head it, so they're preparing a big Prairie. You'll just have to wait like everyone else." There was no mistaking the broad suggestion of gloating in the bobby's words.

"And how long do we have to wait?" demanded Herbie.

"Buggered if I know. But I'm sure they'll tell me when they're ready!"

Herbie snarled an unprintable expletive and left the cab with the cackling of the bobby in his ears.

"These top link drivers think they're royalty and everything must give way to them," laughed the bobby to his mate in the cabin. Then he turned serious, "But they're right this time. These new diesels are bloody dreadful: they're rough at high speeds and can derail over points."

It was another ten minutes before the signal changed, allowing the Riviera into Taunton Station where they had to stop again.

"Now what?" wondered Bill. "Don't they know who we are?"

He sauntered to the platform side of the cab and peered along the platform. The guard was already out, ensuring that no passengers either alighted or boarded the train: it was not timetabled to stop here. The stationmaster appeared, approaching the King.

"I'm sorry, Driver Clifford, you will be held for a while yet. There are two trains ahead of you, and one of them – your relief – is struggling up Wellington bank."

Bill frowned. "Is this normal, sir, on Saturdays? I don't usually have a Saturday duty."

The stationmaster nodded. "And it's getting worse. We were hoping the diesels would speed things up but they're not as reliable as we'd hoped. Summer Saturdays are bad news these days for us here where the four track becomes only double track into the West. Now that things are looking up in the country after the last war, everyone wants to go on holiday in Devon and Cornwall, and of course they take the train. I'm just waiting for the Riviera to require five relief trains on Saturdays; won't be long now, I reckon."

Bill shook his head. "Five reliefs?"

"And I wouldn't be surprised if they put on a sixth soon."

"Blimey! As bad as that?"

"As bad as that! But be assured, we'll get you moving as soon as we can clear this congestion."

"Sir." Bill turned back to his side of the cab. "Did you catch all that, Herbie?"

"Yes, I did. It means we'll be slow up Wellington bank and I'll be shovelling my arse off!"

"When we get the clear from the starter, Herbie, I'll take your shovel for a few minutes to give you a chance to get ready!"

"Ta, Bill; I'd appreciate that. D'you still remember which end of the shovel goes into the fire?"

"Get the tea on, you cheeky bugger!"

They still had fifteen minutes for their tea. Then the starter signal allowed them out of Taunton, and Bill took hold of the shovel and set to preparing the fire. Herbie watched, impressed. *The man hasn't forgotten anything about firing!* As soon as they began to rise into the bank, Bill handed the shovel over to his mate with a grin. "I bet you thought I'd forgotten how to fire, Herbie."

"Never entered my head, Bill!"

"Lying sod!"

They continued to lose time up the bank, held at signals several times before reaching Tiverton Junction, where they were halted once again.

"This is getting ridiculous!" growled Bill. "We're well over seventy minutes down!"

By the time they reached Exeter they had lost another ten minutes, but surprisingly they were able to trundle through Exeter St David's and pick up speed. However, luck was against them when they saw the distant for Newton Abbot. They slowed right down and came to a stop in the station. As they waited, they noticed a Mogul and a large Prairie coupled together, passing on the up line. Bill nudged his fireman and pointed at the two coupled locomotives. "What's the betting they took that relief ahead of us and slowed us so much that Newton found something stronger and took 'em off to send 'em back to Taunton?"

Just as he spoke, an inspector came up to their King. "Just to let you know, Driver, the train ahead of you now has a County and shouldn't be holding you up."

Herbie shook his head, "You always bloody know it, Bill!"

Bill tapped his nose, "You gotta use your nous in this game, Herbie."

"You don't say!"

They didn't have long to wait; the signal lowered and they were off again, rumbling over the points and crossings south of Newton at Aller Junction, where the route to Kingswear left the main line. They were hoping that things would be easier now; much of the summer holiday traffic headed for seaside resorts of Torquay, Paignton and Kingswear, where the ferry took passengers to Dartmouth.

The whole of Torbay was a major holiday destination for thousands, and for most people the railway was still the main means of getting there; there were direct connections not just from Paddington but also from the Midlands, Manchester, Liverpool, and even the north-east. Nevertheless, for Herbie the run was not significantly easier; their next section was over the South Devon banks to Plymouth and firemen definitely had their work cut out because of the gradients. Even the powerful Kings were not permitted to take more than 360 tons on their own. If their load was heavier, as it often was, a pilot would back on at Newton Abbot and firemen of both locomotives would be shovelling hard over Dainton, Rattery and Hemerdon Banks, which would test not only the firemen but the engine condition as well.

However, the Cornish Riviera on this run only had ten coaches and Herbie was familiar with the 1:36 and 1:45 gradients, having tackled them many times already, although the last time had been five months back.

Bill's going to tell me this section was designed by Brunel to run on the atmospheric principle, Herbie grinned to himself as he shovelled. *And he'll add that it was Brunel's most embarrassing error!*

"You realise, Herbie, that this section was designed for the atmospheric system – Brunel's biggest cockup?" remarked Bill.

"Yes, Bill, you've mentioned that five or ten times," replied Herbie. "Can't recall exactly how many."

"You also know that, apart from being a good fireman, you're also damn good at spoiling my fun!"

"Sorry, Bill, I'll try not to do it again."

But the banter ceased as the first gradient up Hemerdon came into sight on the curving line and both men had to concentrate on the task in hand: Herbie on the fire and Bill on the condition of the thirty-year-old engine. The climb initially indicated that neither Herbie's shoulders nor their King's condition showed the slightest reluctance to cope with the demands imposed and their progress continued smoothly. However, the Brent distant signal showed that the following home signal was at stop. Cursing, Bill slowed the train, which was only permitted to crawl into the station there and come to a halt.

"How many stops have we had, Herbie, on our non-stop to Plymouth?" asked Bill. "I've completely lost count. There'll be a fair few letters to the management after this journey, and doubtless we'll get a few enquiries too."

Herbie put his shovel down and began a mental calculation before giving up. "I dunno Bill, I've lost count too. It's been too bloody many."

Just as he spoke, the starter dropped with a clang and they could move off again, and there were no more stops but several signal delays before they finally reached Plymouth North Road, where Bill and Herbie were to book off-duty.

Herbie jumped down to uncouple so that the waiting County class 4-6-0 could back on. They moved away from their coaches and backed through the station towards the shed at Laira, where they left their King to allow the service crew to take over and see to its preparation for their return the following day.

They had just booked off and were leaving the shed for their accommodation when an engineman walked up to them, grinning at the fireman. "Herbie Campbell! Good day, Herbie, haven't seen you for ages. How're things?"

Herbie looked up. "John! What a great surprise!" He turned to Bill. "Bill, this is my old mate, Driver John Walker. John was my driver when I lived up north in Wellington Salop before I met Annie and moved to London."

Bill shook John's hand. "Nice to meet you, John."

"Did you two come down on the Riviera?" asked the other driver.

"Yes, we just got in," replied Herbie. "Why?"

"Bugger of a run, was it?"

"Damn right, it was. How did you know?"

"I was driving your relief in a Warship. We had to fail it and took over a Prairie as pilot to a Mogul at Taunton. We had a sod of a trip too."

"Was it the Mogul or your Prairie that was slow?"

"Neither; they both handled the train well, but it made little difference: the signals over the banks kept us slow. These holiday Saturdays are always causing delays, and it won't stop until we get quadruple track or people start travelling in their new cars!"

***

Back in Plymouth Station, the County had backed on to the Riviera to take it to its final destination at Penzance. Fireman Charles Perkins was looking forward to the run and rubbing his hands in anticipation.

"What are you looking so smug about, Charlie?" asked his driver, Edward Veno.

"How often, Ted, do we get an engine fresh from a sole and heel out of Swindon?"

"Yes, you have a point there, but we're already over an hour down; and this is the Riviera, remember. Then there's our esteemed clients on holiday who don't want to be late at their B and Bs, not to mention the hills and curving route!"

"I know that, of course, but—"

"And don't forget the local trains full for Looe, Newquay, Falmouth and St Ives! They'll all be busy and holding us up, if we're unlucky!"

"Ted, you're a barrel of laughs."

"Just bringing you down to earth, Charlie."

Ted's words appeared prophetic; they had to wait another ten minutes before they were cleared for departure. Once they were through the Plymouth suburbs and over Saltash Bridge, however, Charlie began to feel cheerful again; their County was obviously in top condition and handled the load with ease, at least until they reached Liskeard, where they slowed for a signal check. Here, Ted glanced over to Charlie with a grin on his face, only to receive the two-finger gesture from his fireman.

As they passed slowly through the station at Liskeard, they saw the platform crowded with passengers with their bags, chattels and children, all waiting for the next up train to Plymouth. There were plenty of passengers for local trains waiting at Bodmin, Lostwithiel and Par as well, to provide headaches for the signalmen who, in turn, caused the problems for Ted and Charlie.

"All we need now is a derailment by some emergency driver," muttered Charlie as they approached St Austell. He looked ahead to see the distant against them and shook his head. "Bloody distant's against us now!"

"You got your wish, Charlie," grunted Ted, hiding his amusement. He had expected to be late on Summer Saturdays and knew there was nothing to be done about it. The next stop was at Truro, where passengers for Falmouth left the train.

"Now we might get a clear run, Charlie," Ted informed his fireman. "This last section shouldn't cause too many problems. I've done this run many times and to get into Penzance less than an hour late is an achievement on a Saturday in August, believe me."

It seemed that Ted was right; they had a straightforward run through St Erth but were only a couple of miles before the extensive carriage sidings at Marazion when again they saw a distant signal against them, showing the next home signal was at danger.

"Now that is unusual," observed Ted. "Must be a local passenger moving into the carriage sidings."

They slowed down, expecting the home signal to clear as they came closer, but it stayed firmly horizontal. Coming to a stop, they waited a while but there was no sign of what was causing the delay, and the nearest signal box was some distance away. Ted did not really want Charlie to have to walk to find out what the problem was when the signal could clear at any time.

Both of them stared carefully at the carriage sidings, where the up trains from Penzance were cleaned and remarshalled to their return runs to Paddington, but everything seemed normal as far as they could judge.

"I don't believe this!" growled Charlie. "Here we are, only ten minutes out of Penzance and we aren't allowed in!"

"Yes, I must say that this is a nuisance," admitted Ted. "It's not anything I have experienced before."

Just then the home signal dropped and, thankfully, Ted eased the train forwards again, but a few moments later they slowed once more as the next home signal was at danger. This time they saw the signal bobby leaning out of the window, waving a flag at them. Ted brought the train to a standstill again and walked to the cab side.

"Sorry, Driver," called the bobby, "you'll have a bit of a wait here; time for a brew if you need one."

"Why? What's the difficulty?"

"Tricky derailment just outside Penzance."

"What's derailed?"

"The ten o'clock Paddington. It had a Warship from Plymouth instead of a Castle. The Warship was fresh out of Swindon and when the carriages were withdrawn to Marazion, the Warship moved out and derailed over the points at the station approach. They're tackling it now but it's a heavy bugger and both bogies have come off."

"When do they think we'll be able to proceed?"

"They estimate no more than another half-hour."

"Bugger!" muttered Ted and swung round to Charlie. "These damn Warships seem to be nothing but trouble. I can't think why; they're based on a German locomotive, the V200, which has an excellent reputation over there. It's not like Swindon to cock up a good design!"

"Maybe not," replied Charlie, putting a can of water on the shovel and into the firebox, "but they have."

It was another three quarters of an hour before they were

cleared to steam into their destination, almost two hours over time. Ted drew up at the stopblocks in Penzance station, applied the brakes, and sat down, exhausted. He glanced sympathetically at Charlie, who was perched on his seat with his arms hanging down in similar inactivity, while anxious passengers hurried past to the station exit, followed by porters with their suitcases.

"Summer Saturdays are normally bad, Charlie, but this one's been an absolute nightmare." He shook his head as he filled the details into his notebook.

Charlie looked up. "It's at times like these I look forward to the future, when passengers going on holidays choose to drive their cars!"

Ted nodded his agreement. "Or when the damn diesels are improved sufficiently to take over the jobs they were designed for!" He looked out over the station; a Pannier was shunting some wagons in the dock sidings and a local passenger for Truro was waiting at an adjoining platform with its Mogul steaming gently; the men in the cab were chatting while the fireman was checking the steam pressure and the driver was adding some detail to his notebook before replacing in the little pocket under the roof.

In some ways, mused Ted, *I'll be sad to see the end of steam here: it's been my life for so many years.*

"What will you do, Charlie, when we're fully dieselised?"

"Me, Ted? I'll be a driver with clean hands and a clean collar!"

"And a layer of fat round your belly!" laughed Ted.

Both men knew perfectly well that the diesel and electric locomotives would see the end of steam within a very few years.

19 – Flagging the Change
(Feb 1961)

For more than a hundred years, Crewe had been the engineering citadel of the LNWR, LMS, and the BR's London Midland Region, although Euston had been the headquarters. Crewe was where most of the great locomotives had been built. But the two bay platforms at the south end of Crewe Station regularly featured appearances from its great rival the GWR. By 1897, the GWR had reached Nantwich, only a couple of miles from Crewe, and for passengers' convenience the GWR service between Wellington and Nantwich had been extended to Crewe so that GWR engines were common in the Crewe south bays.

But the rivalry still existed in the minds of the enginemen. The GWR had even built a small two-engine facility at Gresty Lane that acted as a sub-shed of Wellington. But Wellington shed itself, situated between major sheds at Wolverhampton and Shrewsbury, had often been seen as relatively minor and a good place to send elderly engines, therefore useful for implying that Crewe was not worth anything better. LMS and GWR drivers had often teased each other, especially when a huge LMS Pacific found itself near a small and almost life-expired GWR locomotive.

This was the case again when a Jubilee 4-6-0 backed onto a waiting Euston train, and its driver caught sight of an ancient and grimy ex-GWR 2-6-2 Prairie with the letters GWR still faintly visible on its side tanks. He leaned out of his cab and called over to the Prairie driver. "Where to next, mate?"

"Back to Wellington in twenty minutes," came the reply.

"Nah! Back to Swindon scrap siding, I'd say! Your little tank engine's ten years out of date: you've still got GWR painted on yer tanks! The Western Region needs the Midland Region to sort it out!"

"Nonsense! We do alright!"

"Not fer long, mate!"

"What d'yer mean?"

"Yer haven't heard the latest?"

"What latest?"

"We're takin' over yer division."

"What, the whole Wolverhampton Division?"

"Yep; the lot: Birken'ead down ter Banbury."

"I don't believe it; that's our main line to the north!"

"Yer don't 'ave ter believe it, but that don't make it wrong," the driver cackled. "Yer'll all be London Midland men unless yer scarper ter the west!"

"When's all this going to happen?"

"It's on the cards, mate, and then some of yer great Kings'll be ours!"

"You're talking through your hat!"

Just then, the Jubilee fireman said something, and the driver sounded his whistle, waved over to the Western driver, and eased his train away. Driver Edward Howland of Wellington shed looked at his fireman, Hubert Strong, and asked, "Have you heard anything about that?"

"Nope."

"Bugger was just teasing then."

But a few years later there were major regional changes, and the Western Region did indeed lose its whole northern section, although it gained most of the Southern's West Country territory.

***

Driver Lance Hargreaves and Fireman Harry Paisley booked off at the office in Stafford Road Shed in Wolverhampton; they had just brought in a County class 4-6-0 on a Birkenhead to Paddington express and had enjoyed an exhilarating run with it. After the war, many ex-GWR engines were reviewed in Swindon to see whether improvements could be made, and the Counties had all been redrafted and had well repaid the attention spent on them.

Harry watched his driver with a grin as they were both headed for the enginemen's mess for a quick mug of tea before leaving. He had seen Barry Stevens enter the mess just before them and looked forward to the discussion which he knew would come. Driver Stevens was a Salop man and, like several of his colleagues, disliked the Counties. Lance Hargreaves, on the other hand, equally favoured them, even preferring them to Castles if the run involved hills. Harry foresaw an interesting and diverting conversation. He didn't have to wait long.

Barry looked up from his mug. "Good day, Lance, just come in, have you?"

"Hello, Barry; yeah, on the Birkenhead."

"Good run, was it?"

"Excellent, wasn't it, Harry?" replied Lance, looking at his fireman, who nodded his agreement.

"You must have had a Castle."

A smiling Lance shook his head. The listening men began to prick up their ears: this was promising!

"A Hall? Or – surely, not a Grange?"

"Neither."

"Well, it couldn't have been a County: they can't climb hills. A Saint would have done it, but they've all been scrapped. Was it a 47 returning to Acton, or did you get lucky with a souped-up Mogul?"

"Nope. Shall I give you a clue?"

"Go on."

"It was a big two-cylinder 4-6-0 with a man who knows how to drive it. And if you want proof, we left Chester seven minutes behind and arrived in 'hampton with four minutes in hand. We gained eleven minutes on the run."

"Impossible with a County!"

"That's only true if the driver's a Salop man."

There were sounds of amusement from the enginemen; several Shrewsbury drivers were known to be unimpressed with their Counties. Lance waited until the mirth had died down and continued, "A dozen years back George Denton showed me how to get the best out of the Counties. Now they're damn good engines."

"Bollocks!"

"Not a convincing reply, Barry. You'll have to do better than that!"

"Well, I don't like 'em!" Barry finished his tea and stalked out.

"And you never tried to find out why?" Lance called after the disappearing Barry with satisfaction, his gesture followed by a shout of laughter from the group.

***

Just before eight o' clock one morning, a 94xx class Pannier tank with its coaches pulled into its platform at Paddington where numbers of passengers with their holiday luggage were waiting; the boards along the coach roofs proudly proclaimed 'Channel Islands Boat Train'. The train was headed for Weymouth, stopping only at Westbury and Yeovil before Weymouth Harbour Station, where the ferry to Guernsey and Jersey would be waiting.

While the passengers were boarding, at the front of the train, Driver Norman Smith backed his Castle gingerly towards the coaches and Lincoln Courtney, his fireman, waited to couple up. Lincoln lifted his hand and Norman braked the engine as, with a gentle bump, the buffers nudged those of the coach, forcing them an inch or two inwards.

"Righto, Norm!" called Lincoln as he dropped down to couple the engine to its train. Once the couplings, vacuum brake pipe and steam heating pipe were all secured, Lincoln climbed back into the cab and checked the fire. Norman lifted his watch from his waistcoat and checked the time. "Seventeen minutes, Linc. Get the can in!"

Lincoln nodded and lifted the tea can, placed it on his shovel and carefully slid it into the fire, while Norman grabbed his mug and milk. Lincoln withdrew the shovel and the two men filled their mugs, adding milk and sugar, to savour their tea before they packed all away and prepared for departure.

The whistle sounded and Norman eased the train away while Lincoln gazed out at the station.

The dozen coaches were an easy load for their Castle, which had been recently outshopped from Swindon, and Norman was looking forward to a straightforward run. The signals were in their favour as they left the West London suburbs of Acton,

Ealing and Southall, and Norman was able to pick up speed. They were able to race through Slough at sixty mph. Lincoln was leaning on the side of his cab, grinning at the commuters waiting to catch their local train to the City; they passed it with its 81xx class 2-6-2T and ten coaches slowing down to stop at Slough. He leaned over to his driver. "So far, so good, Norm!"

Norman nodded, "Let's hope it stays this way."

They appeared to be in luck: the signals were clear all the way through Reading, and they were able to pick up speed and hurtle on the fast line at almost 70mph.

"I sometimes wonder, Norm, which is best: watching a Castle with its train belting past you at eighty or sitting in the cab with one doing the same!"

"No contest, Linc, not when you're the driver. The feeling of being in control of this engine at our speed is indescribable; you can't beat it! It's the atmosphere of smoke, steam, oil and even the shaking of the cab and seeing the rods whirling round when you glance along. With any luck, we'll be doing this all the way to Westbury before we stop again."

"What about being a diesel driver?"

"I don't know about that, but I once sat with the motorman in the cab of a Southern Electric to Portsmouth running at over eighty; we were running very smoothly, and it was exciting yet totally different. I imagine you could get used to that."

"But it wouldn't have been the same, eh?"

Norm nodded his agreement. "No, it wasn't the same." He paused, pondering, "But you'd have to ask a Southern motorman; I suppose they might claim equal satisfaction."

Lincoln went back to check his fire and threw several shovelfuls of coal where he felt they were needed. He glanced over at his driver as they thundered through Newbury at close to eighty; Norm was sitting on his seat, hand resting on the regulator, a rapt expression on his face.

Lincoln smiled, "You're really enjoying this aren't you?"

Norm turned to him in surprise, "How could you not?"

Lincoln laughed and checked the steam pressure to ensure that Norman had sufficient to keep up the tempo. Much later, he glanced out of the cab to see they were passing Castle Cary, still at some speed. He shook his head in wonderment: the signalmen had been on their side all the way so far. It didn't seem right. When would they be held up? Surely, they couldn't be fortunate all the way? But it seemed that the gods were generous this time; there were no checks until they reached Weymouth dead on time.

To get to Weymouth Quay, their train had to traverse some of the town itself along the tramway, and this final stretch was not the duty of their Castle. They stopped to uncouple so that a Pannier could take the train through the town with railway staff walking alongside to check that all parked cars were clear of the train on the town streets to the ferry terminal.

The two men entered Weymouth shed for a break before returning on a train after their Castle had been turned and serviced.

"It's after trips like the one we just had, Linc, that I will regret changing to diesels," remarked Norman.

***

In the shed at Newport, Driver Llewellyn Hughes walked over to his booked engine, a Mogul which had seen many better days, and grimaced.

"We might have a problem or two today," he told his fireman Ianto Evans. "This engine looks a little worse for wear; we're to top up Swindon's supplies with thirty wagons of good steam coal, and I'm not sure we'll get there."

"Why's that, Mr Hughes?"

"I had this yere engine last week, and she's overdue for servicing."

"I'm sure you'll manage."

Ianto had more confidence in his driver than Llewellyn had in the engine they were to take. Their coal train was waiting in the siding where an 0-6-2T, one of Collett's heavy tank engines, had brought it from the coalfield, and they backed on and waited for the signal to clear them for the Severn Tunnel route. Normally a Mogul in reasonable condition would manage this load without much difficulty but their engine today was not in reasonable condition. The tubes needed cleaning, part of the motion was loose, and Ianto was having trouble keeping up the steam pressure. In short, they struggled with their loaded train to reach the tunnel.

However, once they began the downhill gradient under the Severn, their locomotive began to manage more easily and they increased their speed slightly until Llewellyn decided to slow in case inertia from the train's weight overcame their speed and pushed it to accelerate out of its driver's control. He managed to slow the train to a walking speed then called urgently to Ianto and told him slip out and put the individual handbrakes on half a dozen wagons.

Ianto did so, running past the wagons and dropping their brake levers as he did so, before returning to the cab.

"Good lad!" Llewellyn was greatly relieved. "We could have lost control: the engine's brake is not holding the train."

They reached the bottom of the tunnel and the engine began to put its nose into the climb again. The danger now was a possible snatch which could break a coupling and part the train. If this happened, the rear of the train with the guard would come to a stop and then gradually roll back downhill, picking up speed as it did so and becoming out of control, with possibly catastrophic results. Ianto slipped out to release the brakes on the wagons and enable the engine to pull uphill more easily. Even so, Llewellyn struggled with the Mogul to ensure it maintained a steady, if slow, rate with its train under control for the rest of the run to Swindon.

"I suspect this engine will not be returning after a maintenance check," he remarked as they entered Swindon yard. "She'll be sent straight to the scrap sidings! I wouldn't wish a nightmare run like we've just had on another crew."

***

Unusually, Driver Bill Henderson was looking forward eagerly to his day's work. He had been told that he was to retrain as a driver of the new suburban diesel train formations. He had been a steam man for many years but now, in his early fifties, he was glad of the chance to leave the grime and physical effort required by a steam locomotive cab in his final years of driving.

"I suppose you don't know when you'll be home tonight, Bill?" asked his wife. "You said there's be some – now what was it – track re-alignments which could make you late?"

Bill smiled at his wife. "No, dear, I won't be late and soon you won't need to wash my gear so much. I'm to train on the diesels! I go to work with a clean collar and tie and return with the same and even clean hands!"

His wife laughed in disbelief. "That'd be a first!"

"No, really Marion, I go to my cab; switch everything on; then check all's well in the cab and drive. No hour spent on going round oiling the motion or all the other grimy duties out in all weathers. And at the end of the shift, I switch off, report off-duty and come home as clean as Will does!"

Will was their son, who worked in an office.

"You mean I won't have to buy a new packet of Persil every month to clean your greasy overalls?"

"No, you won't, and just imagine, so many wives all over the country will be rejoicing too when we're all driving diesels!"

"What do the other men think?"

"Most of 'em can't wait to get into diesels. There are a few diehards of course, but there aren't many."

"Diehards? You mean men who like to work in steam engine cabs?" Marion found this hard to believe; she had visited her husband in a cab more than once and was well aware of what the work was like.

"Oh yes, they say they relish the feeling of controlling a 70-ton machine in charge of a train with several hundred people relying on them!"

"But you'd get that in any train! Whether it has a diesel or a steamer in charge."

"Yes, but the atmosphere in a steamer is totally different. I don't quite understand it myself, but there's something about the hard, dirty work, the smell of steam, smoke and oil, all of which can make you feel you've earned some praise, even if you don't get it. There's a bit of pride in it, I think."

"William Henderson, I believe you almost regret having to train on diesels!" Marion mocked her husband.

Bill paused before responding. "D'you know, Marion, you could be right. I think I might miss some parts of the job. Racing through Reading or Westbury with a King in good nick and with fifteen 35-tonners behind you is a great feeling. On the other hand, with an old Mogul in poor condition and a heavy, unfitted goods punching uphill in the pouring rain and sweating that your train won't part from a broken coupling is something – that I won't miss!"

"But that doesn't happen too often, does it?"

"More often than any steam engineman wants, believe me!"

"But then it's fine when you reach the top?"

"Not a bit of it; it gets worse. Then you worry that the weight of the train will overcome your brakes, and it'll force you downhill and you can't bloody stop it!"

"And this won't happen with the diesels?"

"Not when the freights are all vacuum-fitted with every vehicle with its own brakes you can apply from the engine. It'll be far easier."

"Those diehards might be a bit like the sailors in the old sailing vessels who thought that steamships were contrary to God's will!" remarked Marion.

Bill laughed. "I bet they changed their minds when they no longer had to climb the masts in a howling gale to reef the topsails!"

It wasn't long before Bill was sitting in one of the Derby Lightweight diesel DMUs next to the driver as the train left the station. He was listening, bemused, to the sound of the train as it rumbled its way out, sounding more like a car, and when on reaching the end of the platform it changed gear, he laughed out loud.

"What's so funny?" queried the driver.

Bill shook his head in disbelief. "I need to get used to this. I've never had to change gear leaving a station before!"

Within a week of driving practice however, Bill was perfectly at ease with the sounds of a diesel train and had accepted his transfer with equanimity and little regret for leaving the steam cabs he had been familiar with all his working life. Now he ended the day with clean clothing and no oil on his hands, no longer physically exhausted.

20 - The Sun Sets in the West
(Oct 1965)

The days of Western steam were almost over. It was becoming rare to see a Western engine in Wolverhampton where many had once been built and, until recently, repaired; indeed, the whole of the old Wolverhampton Division had been transferred to the Midland Region two years earlier. In fact, it was even uncommon to see an ex-GWR steam locomotive on the Western Region itself as the diesels were taking over. The word had gone out that the Western had imposed a ban on steam from 1st January 1966, by which time they would have scrapped or sold all their steam locomotives. The only exception was the Vale of Rheidol narrow gauge tourist railway in Wales; this had been GWR and then Western Region property since 1948

One day in early summer, Driver Lance Hargreaves, now at Oxley shed since Stafford Road had closed, glanced at the board in the office.

Driver Hargreaves: Grange light engine to Salop to take over the midnight passenger Paddington to Birkenhead, leaving at 5.35 for Chester.

Hmm, no problem there and it will be nice to get his hands on a steamer once more. And, I've been given Harry Paisley again.

He hadn't had Harry firing for him for quite a while and was pleased; they'd got on well. He just hoped their locomotive wouldn't be the Grange he had driven a fortnight back. That was a poor steamer, urgently due for repair, but probably wouldn't get any more attention; there was no interest in wasting money repairing steamers due for scrapping soon now that diesels were becoming more reliable.

The diesel from Paddington might be a Class 52. Lance liked them, although they weren't steamers; some of their problems had been partly ironed out, and they were proving to be useful general-purpose engines. Their main difficulty seemed to be that they were diesel-hydraulic where most other diesels were diesel-electric, which meant that maintenance could be more expensive when the railways were desperately trying to save money.

Still, concluded Lance, *that's a problem for the government thinkers, not for Lancelot Hargreaves.*

He glanced at the fireman standing next to him. "Listen, Harry, you've got an education. Tell me, is 'government thinking' a contradiction in terms?"

Harry laughed. "Ah, Lance, you mean an oxymoron. Yes, I believe it is, just like 'common sense' or 'military intelligence'!"

Lance read further to see that they were to return from Chester with a Black Five on the Margate as far as Oxford then hand the train over to a Southern engine for the south coast. Return Oxford to Banbury on the cushions, then pick up a class 52 diesel engine back to Wolverhampton. *No great problem then, as long as the steamers don't play up.*

"Come on, Harry," Lance called cheerfully to his mate, "we're steaming to Chester on a down Birkenhead."

"What are we steaming on?"

"Grange."

The 4-6-0 ex-GWR Granges had been among the best of the Western's general service engines; developed by the GWR, they were equally at home with fast freights as with express passenger trains and were reliable. They had been built in 1938 and were very popular among GWR enginemen. They were very similar to the Halls but had slightly smaller wheels and were marginally more powerful. But, like most steam locomotives in recent days, their maintenance had suffered from low priority and its consequent unreliability. Most, Lance assumed, would head for the scrap yards within a very short time, but this depended upon the shed being supplied with diesels suitable to take over. Luckily, the number of such diesels was gradually increasing.

Lance was disappointed to find that his engine was in fact the Grange he had disliked; there were so many problems with it, he had not been able to work out which was the worst. The glands were leaking, the regulator was getting very stiff, the outside motion was clanking, it was using more oil than it should, and consequently the steaming was poor, not like what a driver would normally expect from a Grange. Fortunately, both he and Harry were experienced steam enginemen and took the light engine to Shrewsbury to await the express from Paddington.

As expected, it arrived on time behind a Class 52 which uncoupled and moved off back to Coleham shed. They backed their Grange onto the train and while Harry coupled on, Lance looked back down the platform, noting that the number of passengers did not indicate a heavy load and they only had seven coaches. This was a blessing under the circumstances because Lance feared they would have enough trouble with the locomotive in any case. Getting this train to Chester on time was going to demand all of Lance's considerable experience and skill gathered over thirty years. Lance was glad he had Harry with him; he was aware the latter did not have the 'feel' for steam, but he had been Lance's mate for long enough for them to be able to form an effective team in a steam cab.

The guard had given the 'all clear to go' and Lance eased the engine into gentle motion without any apparent complaint. They accelerated northwards past the goods sidings and made good, if not rapid, progress towards Gobowen, where the auto train to Oswestry was waiting for them.

"Seems she's looking forward to being useful again, Lance," remarked Harry as they left again. "She's behaving herself!" He bent down to throw five more shovelfuls down each side of the firebox and three more into the centre. But later, on leaving Ruabon, the engine began to labour and Lance eased the regulator slightly to allow it to pick up again.

"You might have spoken too soon, Harry," grumbled Lance. "She must have heard you."

"I'm sure you'll manage, Lance."

The driver nodded. "I drove a Grange once from Wolverhampton to Oxford on a Margate express with ten corridors on and got her up to seventy. That was about 1956, I think. The Castle due to take the train had been failed at the last minute."

"Seventy miles an hour?" Harry found this hard to credit.

"Yep, and it was no problem either, even with their smaller wheels."

They pulled in at Wrexham half an hour down and with the engine clearly struggling with only a moderate load. Lance was wondering privately whether he should fail this engine or ask for a pilot, but Wrexham shed would probably not have anything suitable, although a small tank engine might be available. Then he thought again: arriving in Chester with a small tank piloting a Grange would be something he would not live down when the enginemen in Chester shed heard about it. He determined to try and bring their Grange in with its train without assistance. Chester men could then fail it, he thought with satisfaction.

"Will you have to fail her?" Harry asked.

"No, Harry, we'll try and get her through on her own."

Harry glanced doubtfully at Lance then, seeing his expression, just nodded and saw to the fire and the steam pressure without comment. He knew his driver. They would soldier on; there was no point in discussing the matter.

It was lucky, he mused as he shovelled, that the next section through Gresford was downhill. That would give them a chance to build up some speed over the flatter section before they had to tackle the run up to Saltney Junction. After that it would be hopefully plain steaming to Chester, where they would book off and hand over their locomotive to some other unfortunates.

The run down Gresford Bank, as they had both hoped, enabled them to get up enough speed to run the few miles across the following plain and even well up past the little halt at Saltney, but once they had joined the main North Wales their Grange began to labour again and even slowed down, only to be nursed carefully and gently through the two tunnels and round the curve into the General Station at Chester and into the bay at Platform Three.

Four yards short of the stopblocks, Lance applied the brake then turned and looked at Harry. "I'm failing her here; she's had her last run. They'll probably tow her to the Chester Midland or

Mold Junction shed, remove her rods, and then she'll join a line of other dead engines destined for the scrapyard."

Harry nodded silently. He knew how much it hurt Lance to have to close the book on an engine, especially one of the eighty Granges. Western drivers had long extolled the qualities of the GWR's big 4-6-0 Kings and Castles (and even latterly the Counties) against engines of the other regions, although they had their detractors too, but the Granges had always been quietly popular among Western enginemen; one had once even remarked that with a fleet of Granges and Collett's 0-6-0 tender engines, one could cope with almost every duty on the Great Western Railway.

There was a gentle bump as one of the BR 2-6-4T tank engines nudged the train at the other end to take it out of the bay platform and on to Birkenhead.

"How are you today, Lance?" A cheerful voice called from the platform as two enginemen climbed up to relieve them and take their Grange to servicing.

"Not the best, Dick," said Lance as he recognised the Chester driver. "I've just had to fail her. You'll have to call the boss for a tow for this Grange. We've lost forty-seven minutes since leaving Shrewsbury on time."

"Time these dinosaurs went to scrap anyway," said Dick, no fan of steam locomotives, "Give me a diesel any day!"

"And up yours too, Dick!" chuckled Lance as he left the cab.

He and Driver Henderson had had many a vigorous argument about the relative merits of driving steam and diesel locomotives.

Lance and Harry walked round to the siding where a Black Five and three more coaches were waiting to relieve the Chester servicing crew. When the express from Birkenhead arrived behind a tank engine, they would back their Five with the strengthening coaches onto the train for the South Coast and take it south to Oxford, where a Southern engine would be waiting to take the train further. Lance hoped the Five, a Chester engine, would give them a satisfactory run; ex-LMS Black fives were generally reliable locomotives and, in Lance's opinion, to be preferred over the BR versions. He sent Harry to the little enginemen's canteen nearby to pick up a couple of buns and mugs of tea.

"You on the Margate today, Harry?" asked another engineman as Harry entered.

"Yeah, that's right Jeff. Why?"

"Word from the London Midland Region is that the Birkenhead to Paddington runs will stop soon."

"What?"

"Yeah, they say that all Chester to London services will be to Euston."

"And the Margate? It's a busy service."

"Only one train a day? I doubt that it'll survive."

"Bloody Beeching!" growled Harry as he picked up his order and left.

Back in the cab, Harry announced, "We're being rationalised, Lance!"

"Rationalised?" Lance was surprised. "What d'you mean, rationalised?"

"I ran into Jeff Willis, and he told me that the Birkenhead to Paddington service was to close soon; all Chester to London trains would be diverted to Euston, and the Margate would probably be discontinued."

"Hmm," muttered Lance.

"You're not surprised?"

"Not entirely, Harry. A hundred years back the GWR wanted to steal some of the LNWR's Merseyside traffic and set up their north-western main line, but it was always far too slow to make serious inroads into Liverpool, taking almost an hour and a half longer."

"I see what you mean," said Harry, mentally comparing the times. He went back to checking the fire and the various other duties while they waited for the Birkenhead to arrive at Platform Two.

Once it had pulled in, they took their coaches out of the siding and then backed them onto the rest of the train and waited for the guard's signal, which came within two minutes, and they were off on time.

Lance, however, was unsure about their Five; as they took the ten coaches up Gresford Bank, their locomotive began to labour. This did not bode well; ten coaches ought to have been a doddle for a Black Five, even up the bank. By the time they had arrived in Shrewsbury twenty minutes down, Lance was sure: their train would be unlikely to reach Oxford unassisted. They lost another nine minutes to Wolverhampton but by Snow Hill they were forty-seven minutes behind time.

He informed the platform inspector that he was failing the engine and asked whether Tyseley had a spare locomotive. They waited while the information was sought, and the inspector brought the surprising yet welcome news that Tyseley did have a steam locomotive which was to go back to Didcot shed light engine anyway. It could take their train, but Lance and Harry would need to crew it.

"No problem, sir, we're on until Oxford anyway," explained Lance, "then Didcot can have their engine back."

The two men did not have long to wait; they caught sight of a clearly ex-GWR tender backing towards their train while they waited in their Five in a siding. Lance's heart surged as he recognised the filthy engine: under all that grime was a Castle!

"We're in luck, Harry!" he chortled.

When the Tyseley crew came over to collect the failed Five, they told Lance and Harry that despite its appearance the Castle was a good engine.

Lance could hardly wait to get his hands on a Western engine in good nick; he took over quickly, eagerly eyeing the dials and levers on the backhead.

Harry was amused at Lance's obvious pleasure, even though he didn't quite share it; he was ready for the diesels. Harry knew all about the so-called 'Romance of Steam'. It existed in the eyes and minds of schoolboys and men who did not work in steam sheds; it was rarely found there.

Men who worked in a steam shed knew very well that work in the cab of a steam locomotive was hard, dirty, and could be very dangerous. There were enginemen who relished the work –

indeed, Lance was one of them – but they were few. A diesel driver could step into his cab and check everything, and within fifteen minutes he could drive off. A steam locomotive from cold would need three or four hours to prepare before it could be driven away to its train. Furthermore, the low pay did not entice young men into steam sheds.

"This is one of the newer Castles, Harry," said Lance, rubbing his hands. "Built by the Great Western after the war. We'll soon see whether what the Tyseley men said was right!"

Harry nodded while checking the steam pressure and peering into the firebox.

"Seems they have prepared her well enough to get her to Oxford, Lance, then she's no longer our problem: Southern blokes will have her."

"Mmm," said Lance in a manner which drew Harry's attention. He stared back. "Mmm?"

"Yeah, Southern blokes, you said."

The guard's whistle sounded, interrupting Harry's thoughts. He looked back to see the flag. "We've got the green."

"Righto." Lance lifted the regulator gently and their engine began to move smoothly off. Ten corridors were nothing for a Castle: fourteen was more like the load they were used to. They steamed out of Snow Hill straight into the long tunnel and then out and past Moor Street Station on their right and through the inner Birmingham suburbs, gaining speed as they accelerated south towards Warwick.

"We might even pick up a few of those lost minutes, Harry!" said Lance, rejoicing at the feel of a GWR locomotive in good condition. He had badly missed this, he realised. Most of the steam locomotives he had driven recently had been either ex-LMS or the newer BR steamers, whereas he had been brought up, so to speak, on GWR engines, on which he felt far more at home. His recent duty on the Grange had been more disappointing than he had realised.

As they drew up twenty minutes later at Leamington Spa, an official was waiting for them on the platform.

"Oh bugger!" muttered Harry.

"Problem?" asked Lance, glancing over at him.

"Possibly. There's an inspector waiting for us."

"'Bugger' seems an appropriate word," agreed Lance as he eased the train gently to a stop.

The inspector came over to them and called up, "You've a slight delay: derailment at Banbury. I estimate you have ten minutes here for a brew."

"Ah, then we shall have to do what we can, sir, won't we?" Lance didn't seem unduly perturbed at the news; he just nodded and took out his tea and sugar to pass them to Harry.

"I must visit the loo, Harry. Keep an eye on things here. Won't be long."

With that he slipped out, leaving a puzzled Harry. Lance hadn't mentioned any urgent need. But as he was back within five minutes, Harry said nothing.

The remaining minutes passed and when they got the guard's signal they took their train out without any fuss. The Castle certainly was in fine fettle. They were in Banbury rapidly and Harry saw the three wagons on a siding next to the main line.

He pointed them out to Lance, "Those are what caused the delay, I'll bet."

"Yeah." Lance had little more to say, and within two minutes they were off, leaving the Paddington route and diverging towards Oxford. Harry looked out as they approached the station to see which Southern engine was waiting for them, but it hadn't arrived yet.

"Damn Southern relief engine's not here, Lance," he called out. "Still, not our problem."

"No, not a problem," agreed Lance, but he made no move to prepare to leave the cab. "Don't worry about cleaning the cab floor, Harry, we're taking her a bit further with the train."

"A bit further?" Harry was startled. "But our shift ends here." He stared at Lance then he laughed. "That stop for a pee! You arranged to take this engine to Didcot, you crafty sod!"

"Didcot, Harry, Didcot? Do they have Southern engines at Didcot? No, mate; we're taking her to Reading! I arranged it in Leamington."

"But why?"

"Think about it: when will we ever get our hands on a Castle again?"

Harry nodded slowly. Driver Lancelot Hargreaves had been a Great Western man and it had called to him again.

Glossary of Technical Railway Terms

Banking engine: An engine at the rear of a train assisting by pushing from behind.

Bobby: railway signalmen. The name derives from Sir Robert Peel's police force. It was also used to refer to railway police. (see also 'Peeler')

Brake van: small van at the end of a goods train from which the guard could apply a brake to assist the driver when slowing the train. In a passenger train, the brake van would be a coach with a section for the guard.

Brighton Line: railwaymen's term for the London, Brighton & South Coast Railway.

Broad gauge: Brunel's original seven foot (and a quarter of an inch) railway gauge for the Great Western Railway, finally abandoned in 1892.

'Coal miners' friend': a term used to describe a driver who was unnecessarily profligate with coal.

Distant: a signal warning drivers about the status of the section following the one they were entering. (see also 'home' and 'starter')

Driver: the man who controls the locomotive.

Down: the direction from London. (see also 'Up')

Express: a fast train with only limited stops.

Fireman: the man who ensures that the locomotive has sufficient energy for the driver to do his job. Earlier commentaries refer to the fireman as a 'stoker'.

Grouping: The Railways act of 1921 grouped the 120 railway companies into four main groups: the Great Western Railway, the London Midland and Scottish Railway, the London & North Eastern Railway and the Southern Railway.

Guard: the official in charge of a train; he was normally at the rear of the train.

Home: a signal indicating whether the next section is clear. (see also 'distant' and 'starter')

Horsebox: a van specially fitted out for transporting horses

Light engine: an engine travelling without a train.

Mixed gauge: a stretch of broad gauge track within which a third, standard gauge rail has been added to allow trains of both gauges to run. (see also Dual gauge)

Motion: the set of coupling and connecting rods linking the driving wheels and the cylinders.

Narrow gauge: broad gauge enginemen of the GWR referred to the standard gauge as 'narrow.'

'On the cushions': enginemen returning from duty and not required to drive a locomotive were permitted to travel in comfort with passengers.

Permanent Way: this is the track and the its foundation which need regular checking.

Pilot engine: engine which would be coupled in front of a train engine and used to assist with a heavy train.

Refuge: a siding to allow a train to back in and pause to allow a more urgent train to overtake.

Relief (train): an extra train needed when a timetabled train is insufficient for the demand.

Salop: railway term for Shrewsbury, based on the original Latin.

Semi-fast: a train which does not stop at all stations.

Single: a locomotive with one large driving wheel on each side.

Shunting: a process whereby railway vehicles were moved about to re-arrange trains. It took place in shunting yards and was done either with a locomotive or by using horses and ropes.

Slip (coach): rear coach of a train which would detach itself to stop at a station, leaving the rest of the train to continue at speed. It needed a special guard.

Slip (trackwork): track formation shorter than a point, allowing a space saving.

Starter: a signal (usually at the end of a platform) to indicate whether a train may move off to the next signal. (see also 'home' and 'distant')

Stoker: early 19th century term sometimes used for a fireman.

Stopblock: a structure at buffer height at the end of a track to prevent further progress.

Stopper: a train which calls at all stations on its run.

Turntable: a large, revolving table in an engine shed. It permits engines to be turned round.

Up: the direction to London. (See also 'down')

GWR Running Sheds

GWR locomotive running sheds all had a shed code printed on the locomotive footplate behind the front buffers. The sheds referred to in the tales are listed.

Town Running Shed codes

Birmingham Tyseley	TYS
Bristol St Philip's Marsh (Pass.)	SPM
Bath Road (Freight)	BRD
Chester	CHR
Crewe Gresty Lane	WLN
Paddington Old Oak Common	PDN
Plymouth Laira	LA
Reading	RDG
Shrewsbury Coleham	SALOP
WolverhamptonStafford Road(Pass.)	SRD
Oxley (Freight)	OXY
Wrexham Croes Newydd	CWND

Collect all the Steaming Into books:

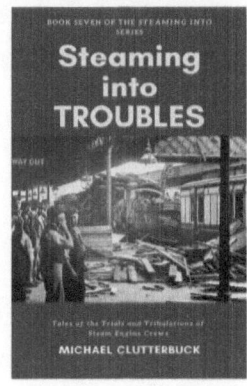

And for those who like reading about crime on the rails, lok no further! Also by Michael Clutterbuck: Rumbles on the Rails.

Retired DI Wolseley nails the one serious criminal he had missed in his career, with no need to abide by police rules of conduct.

A trip on the Irish Mail can have unexpectedly deadly consequences.

www.ingramcontent.com/pod-product-compliance
Lightning Source LLC
Chambersburg PA
CBHW030321080526
44584CB00012B/653